YELLOWSTONE FISHING GUIDE

Robert E. Charlton

A COMPLETE GUIDE
TO THE LAKES AND STREAMS
OF YELLOWSTONE NATIONAL PARK

D1506478

Flying Pencil Publications
Portland, Oregon

Management of Park Fisheries

Yellowstone, America's first National Park, was established in order to preserve its unique natural environment, and to provide an opportunity for future generations of visitors to see and appreciate native plant and animal life as it was found on the wild continent.

Fishing has always played a role in the life of the park, and it is managed in a way that is consistent with the park's primary preservation goal. Fishing by visitors is compatible with the purpose of Yellowstone National Park when it does not deny food that supports the fish-eating birds and animals, and does not impact native fish populations to the extent that their numbers decline.

Fish were first stocked in Yellowstone in the 1890s, and stocking continued up into the 1950s. An enthusiasm for stocking overlooked the impact of hatchery fish upon wild fish populations in the park. By the '50s scientific studies had demonstrated that the native fish of the park were adversely affected by the stocking programs. Pure genetic strains of native cutthroat were becoming hybridized, and competition for food and shelter from hatchery trout was reducing native and wild trout populations.

Regulations to restore or protect fisheries and maintain high quality angling have included manipulating season dates, restricting baits, establishing creel and size limits, and designating certain species or waters for catch and release fishing only. These management practices have improved fish populations, and fishing in Yellowstone today is superior to that found before the restrictions were implemented. Though not required by regulation to do so on all waters, fishermen in Yellowstone are encouraged to preserve the fishing opportunities for future generations by releasing their fish.

Today the fisheries management program within the park is administered by the U.S. Fish and Wildlife Service. Their published objectives are:

- To manage the fishery program as an integral part of the park ecosystem.

- To preserve and restore native species and aquatic habitats; and

- To provide fishermen with high-quality angling for wild fish in natural environments in a manner consistent with the first two objectives.

TOM MONTGOMERY

to be a problem. Backcountry explorers often prefer the month of August for its milder nights, bug-free days, and good fishing.

By late September, hillsides shimmer golden-yellow as aspen tremble in the wind. Waters run low and clear, and the stream angler must be prepared to stalk his prey. This is the favorite time for many park regulars. The summer crowds have thinned and the crisp air crackles with the rapidly advancing fall. A few snows can be expected. By October you can expect sub-zero night temperatures and the first of the heavy snows.

Weather at Yellowstone is notoriously unpredictable and can change rapidly. Snowfalls can occur during any month of the year. A day which begins sunny and mild can develop within a few hours into showers or even mountain shaking, hail spitting thunderstorms.

Even on a mid-summer day hike it's prudent to pack along extra clothing, such as a warm sweater, extra wool socks, and a lightweight rainproof jacket. And don't forget the bug juice.

Effects of the 1988 Yellowstone Fires

America held its breath as the fires of Yellowstone raged in the summer of 1988. Those who had visited the park, or who meant to someday, worried about survival of the park's scenic treasures and abundant wildlife...and wondered what would be left.

The burned areas of the park have now been well surveyed and mapped. Approximately one third of the park was affected by the fires. However, only about half of the affected acreage experienced canopy burn, where needles or leaves and many smaller branches were consumed and trees totally blackened and killed. All patrol cabins are still in place.

It is too early to know with certainty the long term effect of the fires. Fire activity did kill many fish. Dead fish were observed in some small headwater streams, probably victims of chemical changes caused by the fires. Accidental drops of fire retardant in the Little Firehole River and Fan Creek also caused significant numbers of fish to perish. Rapid recovery is expected, and the 1989 angling results were surprisingly good.

Here is what park naturalists and fisheries biologists tell us we can expect:

• **Higher stream flows** on some drainages as a result of the loss of ground cover. This change may continue for many years, until vegetation returns to its pre-fire state. The good news is that the major streams supporting the highest percentage of fishermen (Yellowstone, Madison, Firehole, Gallatin, Gardner, Lower Lamar, and Gibbon rivers) were not impacted to the extent of many smaller headwater streams.

• **Muddy water** as sediment moves downstream. Increased run-off will undoubtably change stream channels and erode banks, especially among the smaller streams such as Lava, Tower, Blacktail Deer, Cache, Hellroaring, and the Upper Lamar River drainage. However, drastically increased siltation has not yet been observed in most streams, *except* after thunderstorms. Waters with a steep gradient seem well able to handle the increased siltation.

• **More deadfall in the streams** than previously encountered. These natural dams should enhance the holding areas for trout but may make fishing more difficult.

• **Increased stream and lake productivity** as a result of nutrients washing into the system from the burned forest soils. The next five years may find fish populations increasing over pre-fire levels in some waters.

• **The visual impact of a burned over area.** Where fires ripped through dense forest with scant undergrowth, blackened snags now stand, though the bark is beginning to slough away to reveal the silver wood beneath. Fire weed is filling in the spaces among the snags, but it will be several more years before full ground cover returns. Forests that had well established ground covers prior to the fire are already green and flowering. Meadows are completely restored to their pre-fire beauty.

Bear Country Precautions

The following is offered to inform, not frighten you. Few people among the millions of Yellowstone visitors have been injured by wildlife, and the majority of them were reaping the harvest of extremely poor judgement. Bear, moose, elk, and bison are powerful, untamed creatures well deserving of your respect. A modicum of prudence will make it most unlikely that you will have a close encounter of the worst kind. Don't try to feed the animals, don't get between a mom and her kids, and keep a respectful distance. Don't keep food in your tent. Common sense stuff. The park service will provide you with pamphlets full of helpful suggestions. Use your head.

Yellowstone is bear country, and noisy hikers are least likely to surprise bears. Loud and continuous talking, wearing a bell, or letting a can of rattling pebbles dangle from your pack as you walk may save you from an unpleasant surprise.

DAVID STOECKLEIN

Fishing Gear Recommendations

There are excellent tackle shops near each park entrance, staffed by clerks who will gladly provide seasoned advice. You really should plan to spend some time in one of the local shops for an up-to-the-minute briefing on what's been taking 'em, and where.

For stream fishing, a small-meshed landing net and a pair of chest waders are recommended. Chest waders offer more versatility than hip boots, allowing you to access the most consistently good sections of both lakes and streams, and providing insulation against cold water temperatures. Waders are not made for walking long distances, so bring good hiking shoes for the trail.

In general, leaders from two to four pounds are usually sufficient for stream fishing, while heavier gear is required for trolling lakes. If you are dry fly fishing, you will find that very small flies and light leaders are necessary later in the season, especially among the wary (and well educated) trout of the park's most accessible waters. Remember that all catch-and-release waters require the use of barbless hooks.

Spin Fishing

On smaller streams, the spinner type lures that do not sink as rapidly seem to do better. At times, a bubble and fly combination is excellent on the lakes and should not be overlooked, especially if you see surface activity and do not have a fly rod. For deep trolling on the lakes, use leaded lines that are color coded so you can keep track of the depth you fish. If you are new to the park and want to troll, ask the guides at the marinas for suggestions. Their advice on where to start and how deep to fish will save you a lot of time.

When fishing from the shoreline on those lakes that are closed to motorized water craft, try the following technique. First, locate some likely looking structure (rocky point, drop off, inlet, etc.) and wade out as deep as your waders permit. Use one of your heavier lures (Fjord Spoons work well), and cast it as far as you can. Count until your lure reaches the bottom, then reel it in. On the next cast, allow the lure to sink, but begin retrieving a few numbers before your lure reaches the bottom. With this method, you will be fishing close to the bottom and can cover the depths efficiently. This method has proved especially effective for taking lake trout and the big cutthroat of Heart Lake.

A good technique to try when fishing the streams is to cast a small spinner upstream, reeling it in just a bit faster than the current.

THE BASIC SPINNING OUTFIT

Medium weight ($6^1/_2$ or 7 foot) rod with six pound test line on an open or closed face spinning reel.

Several plastic bubbles for casting flies.

Number 4, 6, and 9 Panther Martin spinners in yellow, black, or red colors.

Number 2 Mepps spinners in gold and silver (gold seems to do better with cutthroat, silver with rainbow).

Daredevils and Spoons in the smaller sizes ($1/_4$ to $1/_2$ ounce). Red and white, bright orange, copper and brass are favorite colors, especially on Yellowstone Lake.

Assorted jigs ($1/_{16}$ to $1/_4$ ounce), various colors.

Assorted wet flies, with and without wings.

Fly Fishing

Bring leaders varying between 1 1/2 pound to three pounds and good fly dope to keep the dry flies on top of the water. A float tube and neoprene waders make a dandy outfit for exploring the fishable lakes.

Fly patterns can be obtained at most of the local tackle shops at the entrances to the park and also within the park at several of the larger stores. Be sure to ask about the hatches currently taking place or about to occur.

If you are in the park around July 15, the stonefly hatch will be proceeding up the Hayden Valley toward Yellowstone Lake. Terrific fly fishing with stonefly imitations begins around that time.

THE BASIC FLY OUTFIT

An 8 1/2 foot fly rod with size 6 or 7 line with both floating double taper and sinking weight forward.

DRY FLIES — Sizes #12 through #18:

Adams	Ginger Quill	Gray Hackle Yellow
Light Cahill	Olive Dun light	Olive Dun dark
Renegade	Royal Wulff	Poly- wing spinners
Sofa Pillow	H & L Variant	Green Drake
Humpy	Quill Gordon	Blue Dun
Elk-hair Caddis	Kings River Caddis	

A good grasshopper imitation (Dave or Whit's Hopper),

WET FLIES AND NYMPHS — Sizes #4 to #12:

Muddler Minnow	Zug Bug	Yellow Grey Hackle
Montana Nymph	Otter Nymph	Renegade
Black Nymph	Bitch Creek	Mormon Girl
Ginger Quill	Woolly Bugger	Leadwing Coachman
Midge Pupae	Caddis Pupae	Black Woollyworm
Olive Woollyworm	Gold Ribbed Hare's Ear	

6

FISHING REGULATIONS

Fishing regulations are frequently revised to respond to changing conditions. Regulations vary greatly from area to area within the park.

Be certain to get a copy of the most recent regulations upon entering the park. All anglers twelve years of age and older are required to obtain a fishing permit prior to fishing park waters.

Permits, maps, and regulations are free and may be obtained at the entrance gates. Ranger stations have the necessary permits and area maps. The park rangers are there to assist you, and you should feel free to turn to them for information concerning park regulations or current fishing, boating, and hiking conditions.

Yellowstone National Park fisheries are managed according to species rather than on a water by water basis. *At this writing*, the following species restrictions are in effect:

Cutthroat trout are restricted to catch and release fishing throughout the park, *except* in Yellowstone Lake, in portions of the Lamar River and its tributaries, and in the Soda Butte Creek Drainage. Check current regulations for catch and size limits.

Grayling are restricted to catch-and-release throughout the park with no exceptions.

Rainbow trout are restricted to catch and release throughout the park except for the Soda Butte Creek Drainage, and the Gardner River and its tributaries.

Brown Trout are available to keep at a rate of two fish per day, any size, except in the Madison, Firehole, and Gibbon River below Gibbon Falls, where keepers must be under 10 inches, and in the Lewis River below Lewis Falls to Lewis Canyon, where fishing for browns is restricted to catch and release only.

Mountain Whitefish may be kept at a rate of two fish per day, any size.

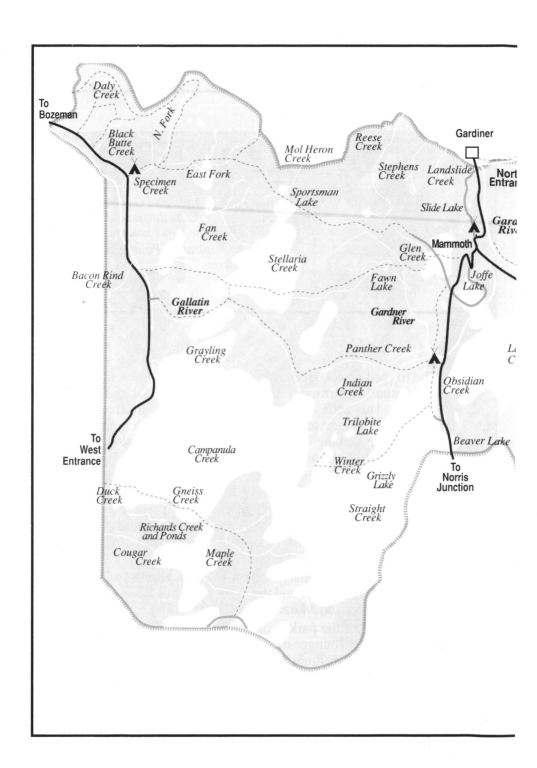

ZONE 1

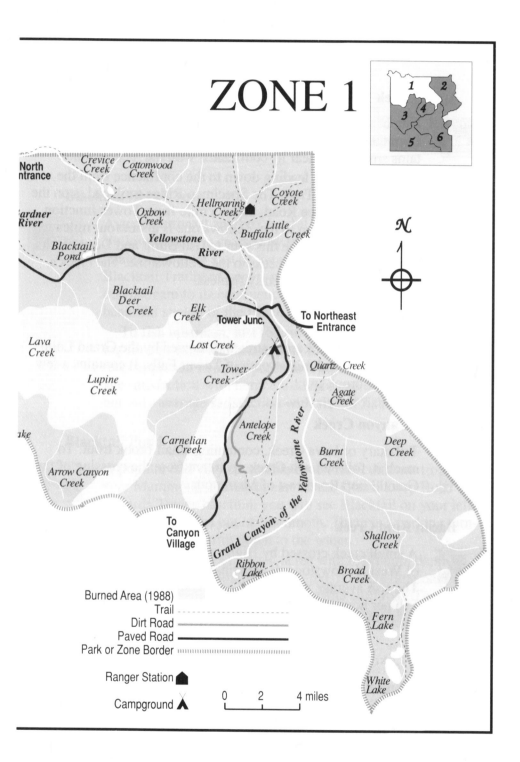

Burned Area (1988)
Trail
Dirt Road
Paved Road
Park or Zone Border

Ranger Station 🏠
Campground ⛺

0   2   4 miles

Broad Creek

A substantial brook trout creek that flows out of the Fern Lake/White Lake basin beneath Stonetop Mountain. It enters the Grand Canyon of the Yellowstone from the east.

You can reach the upper stretch of Broad Creek by following the Wapiti Lake Trail. The trail can be taken from the Upper Falls or Artist Point across the river from Canyon Village. Broad Creek supports a population of cutthroat trout which average ten inches. Landing rates under one fish per hour are reported, with excellent satisfaction with the experience and the size and numbers of fish caught. The Wapiti Lake Trail is frequently used as a means to access the off-trail geothermal sites of the Mirror Plateau.

Burnt Creek

A tributary of Deep Creek, accessed by way of the Specimen Ridge Trail. It joins Deep Creek just before its confluence with the Yellowstone. To reach both creeks, take the Specimen Ridge Trail into the canyon to the junction of the Agate Creek spur trail, following the spur about four miles to Agate's confluence with the Yellowstone. Then proceed upstream along the Yellowstone less than a mile to Deep Creek. Following Deep Creek upstream, you will find Burnt Creek pouring in from the right. Like Deep and Agate, Burnt Creek has a population of small trout in its lowest reach.

Campanula Creek See Duck Creek.

Carnelian Creek

A tributary of Tower Creek, flowing north off Dunraven Peak. It joins Tower about four miles southwest of Tower Falls Campground. A trail heading southwest from the camp reaches Carnelian at about mile four. Both Tower and Carnelian contain rainbow and brook trout.

Cottonwood Creek

Tributary of the Yellowstone near the north boundary, offering excellent fishing for small cutthroat. It enters the Yellowstone east of the Blacktail Trail Bridge. Turn right onto the Yellowstone Trail after crossing the river. Cottonwood Creek is the second stream you will come to. Anglers rate their experience on Cottonwood as excellent, with a landing rate of nearly two fish per hour.

Coyote Creek

A tributary of Hellroaring Creek offering good fishing for pan-size cutthroat. It can be reached by the Coyote Creek Trail or the Hellroaring Trail. Both trails lead into the Absaroka Primitive Area of the Gallatin National Forest. A Montana state license is required to fish Coyote beyond the park boundary. The prominent cone to the west is Hellroaring Mountain, one of the few granite peaks in the park.

Cougar Creek

A cutthroat stream with excellent angler ratings. Cougar and nearby Maple Creeks can be reached by following the directions to Duck Creek, but instead of following the road to the left at the park boundary, follow the car tracks to the right which lead to Maple Creek.

Cougar used to be joined by Maple Creek just upstream from the highway crossing. Currently it appears to disappear into a meadow. To reach it, follow Maple Creek upstream.

The Gneiss Creek Trail crosses an upper stretch of Cougar Creek. Gneiss Creek Trail, heads north from the West Entrance Road between West Yellowstone and Madison Junction, about seven miles from the West Entrance.

Anglers have given this creek excellent ratings for total experience and numbers of fish caught. Landing rates are generally less than one fish per hour, with a catch averaging eleven inches.

Crevice Creek

Tributary of the Yellowstone above Knowles Falls, providing fair fishing for pan-size trout, probably cutthroat. To reach it, follow the Blacktail Trail to its junction with the Yellowstone River Trail. Bear left at the junction, keeping an eye out for the trail sign for Crevice Creek and the ranger station.

Daly Creek

A small mountain stream in the lightly visited northwest corner of the park. It joins the Gallatin River after meandering through a pretty valley dotted with aspen groves and offering handsome mountain vistas.

Daly contains pan-size cutthroat trout and can be reached by way of the Daly Creek Trail, which heads at the confluence of Daly Creek and the Gallatin River along Highway 191, thirty miles north of West Yellowstone.

Deep Creek

Joins the Yellowstone from the west in the lower Grand Canyon area. Small trout can be found near the creek's confluence with the Yellowstone. Otherwise, the creek is fishless. To access the confluence, follow the Specimen Ridge Trail east from the Northeast Entrance Road. Take the spur trail that leads down to the river (at the mouth of Agate Creek, a four mile hike), then proceed upstream along the Yellowstone less than a mile.

Duck Creek

A fine, meandering meadow stream with some deep holes holding good size trout. Duck Creek and its tributaries contain brown, brook and rainbow trout. At times fishing here has been rated excellent.

To reach the creek, follow Highway 191 north eight miles from West Yellowstone. Watch for a sign on the right. Turn right at the sign and keep right one mile until you reach the telephone line that marks the park boundary. The road to the left leads to a parking area and the head of Gneiss Creek Trail.

The trail follows the north bank of Duck, skirting most of the marshy areas. Plan to get wet if you aren't wearing rubber boots.

Campanula, Gneiss, and Richards creeks join to form Duck about one mile upstream from the head of Gneiss Creek Trail. At the confluence, Campanula Creek is to the left and Richards Creek is to the right. The main trail follows Gneiss Creek, crossing it and continuing on into the beautiful Madison Valley. There is often a designated camp at Gneiss Creek.

There are some small springs emptying into Duck Creek, so be careful to remain on the forks containing the most water. Gneiss Creek joins from the east, and the three tributaries form a semi- circle with Duck Creek receiving the water. Richards Creek is the better tributary to fish, although during spawning season the others will hold large fish.

Fly anglers should come prepared with small dry flies (especially caddis), and dragonfly and damselfly nymphs. Be sure to bring grasshopper imitations in late July and August.

Angler satisfaction with Duck Creek is often reported as excellent in all rating categories (experience, size, and numbers of fish caught).

Elk Creek

A good brook trout stream, crossed by the Grand Loop Road west of Tower Junction. It is joined by its larger tributary, Lost Creek, about two miles downstream of the Garnet Hill trailhead. The Garnet Hill Trail then parallels Elk to its confluence with the Yellowstone. Pan-size brook trout are found in both Elk and Lost, with larger fish available in the lower section near the Yellowstone.

Fan Creek

A small spring-fed creek with a good reputation. It enters the Gallatin close to Highway 191, approximately twenty-two miles from West Yellowstone. It contains cutthroat and rainbow trout averaging ten inches.

The Fawn Pass Trail crosses Fan Creek and follows it a short distance, providing some access. Angler surveys have reported excellent ratings both for size of the fish and numbers caught. Landing rates of more than one fish per hour have been reported.

Fawn Lake

A marshy lake in the North Gardners Hole area, south of the Fawn Pass Trail about three miles west of the trail's inter-section with the Glen Creek Service Road. The lake is visible a short distance south of the trail.

It supports a population of brook trout averaging ten inches, with reported landing rate of over two fish per hour. Anglers report excellent satisfaction with their experience here, with size of fish, and with numbers caught. Marshy terrain makes fishing portions of the lake difficult, and aquatic plant growth makes fishing from shore almost impossible in late summer.

Fern Lake

A cutthroat lake north of Pelican Valley, above the northern end of Yellowstone Lake. It is reached by following the Pel-ican Creek Trail to the Astringent Creek Trail, which continues north to Fern. The approximate distance is eleven miles one way, beginning at the Pelican trailhead at the end of the service road about three miles from Fishing Bridge on the East Entrance Road. The lake covers about ninety acres, with maximum depth twenty-five feet. It is set in a heavily wooded area, with hot springs near the east shore. A return trip by way of the Pelican Creek Trail (about sixteen miles), leads past some interesting geothermal features, including The Mud-kettles and The Mushpots. Other fishable waters in the area include Pelican Creek, Broad Creek, and White Lake.

Fern Lake supports a small population of cutthroat trout that apparently immigrated into the lake from Broad Creek. The western and southern shores of the lake were affected by the 1988 forest fire, so you may want to check on recovery status before planning a trip.

Gallatin River

Headwaters of one of Montana's major fisheries. Though the most famous portion of the river is well beyond park boundaries, the headwaters offer good fishing, especially in the back-country stretch.

The river forms as the outlet of Gallatin Lake, below Three Rivers Peak. The Big Horn Pass Trail provides access to the upper stream, which meanders through a big meadowland.

The meadow portion of the river is easy to fish and easy to wade, with undercut banks, plenty of good holes, and unlimited backcasting room. To reach the trail, follow Highway 191 north from West Yellowstone about twenty-two miles to a spur road that leads east about a mile past Divide Lake.

Within the park, the Gallatin contains primarily cutthroat, rainbow, and whitefish averaging twelve inches. Fishing success has been variable, with the best catches reported in the more inaccessible areas. Most anglers, however, fish along the roadside, reporting catches of more than one fish per hour.

Anglers rate this river above average in size of fish, number of fish caught, and over-all angling experience.

Gardner River

A good tributary of the Yellowstone River, formed in the high country below Electric Peak near the north boundary, and joining the Yellowstone at Gardiner.

The Gardner offers good fishing for small, plentiful brook trout above Osprey Falls, where there are special regulations that allow children under eleven to use worms as bait. Below the falls, which head the spectacular Sheepeater Canyon, the river attracts more serious anglers, challenged by its pocket water and larger fish.

Sportsman Lake Trail and Fawn Pass Trail both cross the the upper backcountry waters. Howard Eaton Trail provides easy access from Indian Creek Campground north into the Gardners Hole area. The lower river is closely followed by the Grand Loop Road and the North Entrance Road.

The lower river contains brook, brown, rainbow, and some cutthroat trout. Nymph fishing can be effective here throughout the season. Grasshopper imitations work well in late summer. Browns from the Yellowstone River enter the Gardner on their spawning run in fall. Check regulations closely for closures related to this migration.

Anglers land fewer than two fish per hour, assigning an above average rating for number of fish caught and over-all experience, and average satisfaction with the sizes landed. Eighty percent of the fishing pressure occurs below Osprey Falls. Above the falls, regulations allow children eleven and under to use worms as bait.

Glen Creek

A small tributary of the Gardner River with easy access from the Grand Loop Road and the Sportsman Lake Trail. It offers fair fishing for pan-size brook trout. Anglers rate their experience on the creek above average, but indicate dissatisfaction with the numbers and sizes of fish caught.

Gneiss Creek See Duck Creek.

Grayling Creek

A spring-fed stream that flows into Hebgen Lake near West Yellowstone. Highway 191 parallels the creek for several miles, beginning about eight miles north of town. Whitefish, rainbow, cutthroat, and brown trout can be taken here, and there is a late fall spawning run of big browns from Hebgen Lake.

Upstream a few miles beyond the highway where the terrain flattens out, the creek has carved deeper holes where larger resident trout may be found. For about three miles above Grayling Falls the stream sees little angling pressure and can be pretty good. Smaller fish are characteristic of the upper waters, with the highest reaches too shallow to support many trout.

Grayling is difficult to fish due to willows and boggy conditions. Landing rates of over one fish per hour are reported. Over-all experience ratings are average, as are the ratings for numbers and size of fish caught.

Grizzly Lake

A long, beautiful lake nestled between two ridges, offering excellent fishing for brook trout to ten inches.

It is reached by a strenuous two mile hike on the Grizzly Lake Trail, which heads west off the Grand Loop Road about eight miles north of Norris Junction. A landing rate of almost two fish per hour has been reported, with excellent ratings for over-all experience and numbers caught, but only average rating for size of fish. The lake is fed, and drained, by Straight Creek.

Grizzly is in an area of the park that was severely affected by the 1988 fires, so you may want to check on its recovery status before planning a trip.

Hellroaring Creek

A cutthroat stream, tributary of the Yellowstone in the Black Canyon stretch, entering the river from the north. The Garnet Hill Trail at Tower Junction will take you to a footbridge across the Yellowstone.

If you can withstand the temptation to fish the Yellowstone, continue on the trail until you reach the Hellroaring Creek Trail. You can fish downstream or upstream from this point. The trail parallels the creek upstream, so access is no problem. There is a footbridge across the creek at the trail junction and another one-half mile above the ranger station. There is usually a designated camp across from the ranger station. The prominent peak visible from the trail is Hellroaring Mountain, one of the park's few exposed granite peaks.

Average size of the cutthroat is about ten inches, with landing rates around two fish per hour.

True to its name, Hellroaring Creek is often high until mid-July. Hellroaring Creek (and trail) continue beyond the park boundary into Montana's beautiful Absaroka Primitive Area (where a Montana fishing license is required).

Angler satisfaction with over-all experience on the creek is excellent, especially for those who hike to the upper stretches.

Maple Creek

A brook and brown trout stream which receives a migration of larger fish from Hebgen Dam in its lower stretch.

To reach Maple, follow Highway 191 north eight miles from West Yellowstone. Watch for a sign on the right, turning right at the sign and keeping right one mile until you reach the telephone line that marks the park boundary. At the boundary, a road to the left leads to the Duck Creek parking area. Car tracks to the right lead to Maple Creek.

Maps to the contrary, Maple Creek no longer joins Cougar Creek. Cougar now disappears into a meadow, and it is Maple that Highway 191 crosses. The Gneiss Creek trail crosses Maple Creek upstream, where there is often a designated campsite.

Mol Heron Creek

A small creek formed partially by the outlet waters of Sportsman Lake.

To fish the creek, follow the Mol Heron Trail, which branches off the Sportsman Lake Trail east of the lake. For complete road and trail directions, see Sportsman Lake. Mol Heron has offered good fishing for pan-size cutthroat trout for those who are willing to make the hike. However, in April of 1990 gasoline from leaking underground storage tanks located just outside the park boundaries found its way into the creek. The extent of damage resulting from this spill had not been determined as we went to press with this guide.

Obsidian Creek

A good brook trout stream, with special regulations that allow children eleven and under to fish with worms as bait. Obsidian Creek parallels the Mammoth-Norris Road from the Grizzly Lake Trailhead to Indian Creek Campground. Near the campground, at Sevenmile Bridge, Obsidian enters the Gardner River.

The creek contains small brook trout, with most angling activity occurring below the confluence of Straight Creek (outlet for Grizzly Lake). A lot of fish are caught here, and anglers report excellent over-all satisfaction with the experience. Satisfaction with size of the fish has been rated above average. Landing rates of over two fish per hour are often reported.

Oxbow Creek

A small mountain stream, tributary of the Yellowstone in the mid-Black Canyon stretch. It contains pan-size brook trout near its confluence with the Yellowstone, but is fishless upstream.

Panther Creek

A brook trout stream near Indian Creek Campground, with special regulations that allow children eleven and under to use worms as bait.

Panther flows into the Gardner River about one-half mile north of Indian Creek. The Big Horn Pass Trail follows the stream for several miles, providing access.

Panther offers fair fishing for brook trout averaging seven inches. Anglers give this stream an average rating for over-all experience and numbers of fish caught, a below average rating for size of fish caught.

Quartz Creek

A small mountain stream which flows into the Yellowstone from Specimen Ridge southeast of Tower Falls. Recent stream surveys suggest it offers marginal habitat and limited fisheries potential.

Reese Creek

A tributary of the Yellowstone River, joining the Yellowstone north of Gardiner where the Yellowstone River forms part of the park boundary. A park road heading north from Gardiner provides access to the stream.

Reese supports a small population of cutthroat and brown trout. At this time it is being closely monitored to determine ways to protect the fishery. Nearby Stephens and Landslide creeks are similar, but catch data is unavailable.

of Mammoth, reaching the lake in eleven miles. The west end of the trail can be picked up at Specimen Creek, twenty miles north of West Yellowstone off Highway 191. The hike up Specimen Creek is especially attractive, past aspen groves and scenic meadows.

Anglers have given Sportsman Lake excellent ratings for the experience and numbers of fish caught. They report a landing rate of over one fish per hour. The lake is in an area of the park that experienced canopy burn during the fires of 1988, so you may want to check its recovery status before planning a trip.

Stellaria Creek

A tributary of the East Fork Fan Creek, north of the Fawn Pass Trail. Recent stream surveys indicate an absence of catchable trout.

Stephens Creek See Reese Creek.
Straight Creek

A well regarded brook trout stream, flowing into the south end of Grizzly Lake and out the north end of the lake.

Below Grizzly Lake, Straight Creek is joined by Winter Creek approximately two miles from the Mount Holmes Trailhead on the Grand Loop Road. The Grizzly Lake Trail provides access to both streams.

Both creeks contain brook trout averaging nine inches. Anglers have rated the fishing excellent in all categories (experience, size and numbers). Landing rates of over two fish per hour have been reported.

Tower Creek

Offers good fishing for brook and rainbow trout in the Tower Falls Campground area. A trail heading southwest from the campground follows the creek upstream to its junction with Carnelian Creek.

The catch average is ten inches, with the size of the fish decreasing the higher you fish. The landing rate is over one fish per hour. Angler satisfaction is rated excellent in all categories.

Trilobite Lake

A brook trout lake, unnamed on most maps, located at the western end of Winter Creek Meadow along the Mt. Holmes Trail.

Little information is available regarding angler success. The Winter Creek Trail area was severely affected by the 1988 fires, though the meadow around the lake seems to have been untouched. You may want to check the status of recovery before planning a trip.

White Lake

Headwaters for Broad Creek. Originally thought to be barren of fish, recent aquatic surveys have revealed a developing cutthroat fishery. Access to the lake is by way of the Astringent Creek and the Pelican Creek trails. Pelican Creek trailhead is at the end of the service road about three miles from Fishing Bridge on the East Entrance Road.

Winter Creek See Straight Creek.

Yellowstone River (Inspiration Point to north boundary)

One of America's largest, wildest, and best trout streams, flowing a total of seventy miles within the park. This portion of the river includes the Grand Canyon of the Yellowstone as well as the lower Black Canyon.

The Grand Canyon of the Yellowstone offers challenging fishing for some of the river's biggest fish. The number of anglers willing to make the 1500 foot descent is on the increase. Angler use of the Canyon stretch has doubled since 1976, and fish per hour landing rates have declined from almost four trout per hour to around one.

The most popular portion of the canyon is between Inspiration Point and Quartz Creek, where the river is accessed by the Seven Mile Hole Trail and Howard Eaton Trail. Seven Mile Hole Trail is especially scenic, heading near the Glacial Boulder above Canyon Village Campground. There is ample parking, and the trail is easy to find and well maintained.

The Grand Canyon is steep and the water swift, so caution is advised. Plan on a vigorous outing if you intend to go in and out the same day. When the stonefly hatch is on, the fish can literally wear you out. In this section, the Yellowstone can seldom be crossed by wading except during low water, and then only in a few places. The river emerges from the canyon near Tower Falls (and campground), powerful and fast, but fishable.

Within a couple of miles, the Yellowstone enters the Black Canyon, which extends for twenty miles. Though less spectacular than the Grand, it is easier to access—more of a hike through sagebrush and juniper (one to four miles) than a climb. Wear good hiking boots, however, and leave your waders behind. Black Canyon water includes a challenging fast-water mix of runs and rapids, numerous cascades, and a full-blown falls, as well as some big deep pools. Cutthroat trout predominate here, though there are also rainbow, brook trout, and whitefish. The average size of the fish varies between twelve and fifteen inches, weighing one to two pounds. Fishing is rated good to excellent, with best catches in the less accessible stretches.

The most consistently successful flies used here match the stonefly nymphs which are found in the stream year around. Bring a variety of sizes, both black and gold. Dry flies can also be effective, especially during the salmonfly hatches from June to September. This portion of the river can be reached by several trails, including the Yellowstone River Trail, Blacktail Trail and Garnet Hill Trail. For information about these and other fishing trails into this area, inquire at Tower Junction. Anglers fishing the canyons should consider carrying a sleeping bag, extra rations, and the necessary permits, just in case good fishing draws you further from the road than originally planned.

The lower section of the Yellowstone, between Knowles Falls and the north park boundary, contains cutthroat, rainbow, brown, and brook trout as well as whitefish, with some catches over eighteen inches. To access this stretch, follow the Yellowstone River Trail which heads at Gardiner (North Entrance), the Blacktail Trail from the Grand Loop Road east of Mammoth, or the park road following the boundary north from Gardiner.

Over-all satisfaction with the Yellowstone River is above average to excellent in all categories. The average length of fish landed has slipped to about fourteen inches, still impressive but an inch less than the previous survey reported.

ZONE 2

*The Lamar River and
Middle Creek watersheds
east of Sylvan Pass.*

This is an area of rugged mountains and wide open valleys. The Lamar River is the central feature, collecting water from a vast wilderness area. It is best fished after the early summer snow melt. The Lamar is easily influenced by storms, which cause discoloration and poor fishing.

Slough Creek, a tributary of the lower Lamar, is a favorite of park anglers. It flows through a broad grassy meadow within easy hiking of the Northeast Entrance Road.

The scenery in this area is outstanding even by Yellowstone standards, with the Beartooth Range and Absaroka peaks dominating the view. Elk bison, antelope, and deer winter here, and spring and fall are good seasons for wildlife watching. Mosquitoes thrive in these meadows and valleys usually until late July.

This zone is reached via the Northeast Entrance Road between the entrance and Tower. The Middle Creek watershed is accessed by the Grand Loop Road from Fishing Bridge to East Entrance Road. There are campgrounds at Slough Creek and Pebble Creek.

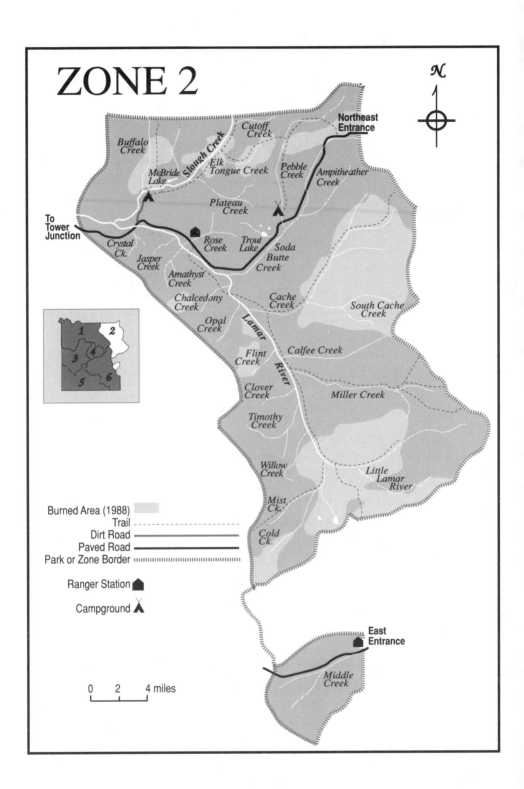

ZONE 2

N

Buffalo Creek

Slough Creek

Cutoff Creek

Northeast Entrance

Elk Tongue Creek

Pebble Creek

McBride Lake

Ampitheather Creek

Plateau Creek

To Tower Junction

Crystal Ck.

Rose Creek

Trout Lake

Soda Butte Creek

Jasper Creek

Amathyst Creek

Chalcedony Creek

Cache Creek

South Cache Creek

Lamar River

Opal Creek

Flint Creek

Calfee Creek

Clover Creek

Miller Creek

Timothy Creek

Willow Creek

Little Lamar River

Mist Ck.

Cold Ck.

Burned Area (1988)
Trail ----------
Dirt Road —————
Paved Road ——————
Park or Zone Border ||||||||||||||||||||

Ranger Station

Campground

0   2   4 miles

East Entrance

Middle Creek

1 2
3 4
5 6

Amphitheater Creek

A tributary of Soda Butte Creek near Pebble Creek Campground. It offers limited fishing for pan-size cutthroat. Amphitheater flows into Soda Butte Creek about one mile above the campground. Thunderer Cutoff Trail begins almost at the confluence, heading west across The Thunderer Mountain.

Buffalo Creek

A tributary of Slough Creek, offering good fishing for pan- size cutthroat. Buffalo Creek empties into Slough Creek near the campground. It offers good fishing for pan-size cutthroat.

Cache Creek

A major tributary of the Lamar River, offering excellent fishing for cutthroat trout averaging eleven inches. The Cache Creek Trail follows the stream to its headwaters and beyond, crossing the Absaroka Range at Republic Pass. The trail heads northeast from the Lamar River Trail a little more than three miles beyond the Soda Butte Creek Bridge. The first two miles are carved into the hillside high above Cache Creek. The trail descends to Cache near Wahb Springs, which emits a noxious hydrogen sulphide gas and should be avoided.

The Cache Creek watershed was severely affected by the 1988 fires. Check on the status of this area before planning a trip.

Cache Creek, South

A good tributary of Cache Creek. Anglers have reported excellent satisfaction with over-all experience here and number of fish caught, and above average satisfaction with size of fish. Landing rates of over two fish per hour have been reported.

This area was severely affected by the fires of 1988, however, so check on recovery status before planning a trip.

Cache Creek and Miller Creek, both of which offer excellent fishing. If the upper Lamar is your destination, be aware that there is no bridge across Cache Creek, which can run high throughout June. Buffalo are often sighted in the area.

Best fished later in the summer, the Lamar River is one of the last streams to clear following spring runoff, and it is often discolored by local thunder storms. Cache, Miller, and Soda Butte creeks are all good alternatives when the Lamar is too muddy to fish.

Fishermen rate the Lamar excellent to above average for over-all experience and for numbers and size of fish. Landing rates are above one fish per hour. Angler success and the average size of trout landed has increased since the implementation of catch and release regulations in portions of the river.

The fires of 1988 burned through sections of the Lamar Trail in the vicinity of the Cache Creek confluence, and in the headwaters area from Willow Creek on up. Check the status of the area before planning a trip.

Little Lamar River

Near the end of the Lamar River Trail, joining the Lamar about a mile from the Cold Creek Patrol Cabin. See Cold Creek for additional information.

The Little Lamar has offered fair fishing for pan-size cutthroat trout. It flows through an area that was severely affected by the fires of 1988. Check on recovery status prior to planning a trip.

McBride Lake

A beautiful twenty-three acre lake situated in grizzly country off the Slough Creek Trail. It offers excellent fishing for cutthroat trout before a late summer algal bloom slows the action. You will need a topographic map to find it.

To reach McBride, follow the Slough Creek Wagon Trail northeast from Slough Creek Campground. The old road climbs through forest for about two miles before reaching Slough Creek in its meadow setting. McBride is above the meadow to the northeast. This bushwhack includes a fording of Slough Creek, which can be high and fast throughout June. McBride Lake is closed to camping due to the presence of bears.

Anglers report high landing rates and excellent satisfaction with McBride in all survey categories.

Middle Creek

A good trout stream, accessed by the East Entrance Road throughout much of its run through the park. If you are heading east toward the entrance after leaving Yellowstone Lake, you will spot Middle Creek on the right just after crossing Sylvan Pass.

Middle Creek supports rainbow and cutthroat trout averaging ten inches in length. Anglers report excellent satisfaction with over-all fishing experience here, above average satisfaction with number caught and size of fish landed.

Miller Creek

Tributary of the Lamar, offering excellent fishing for pan-size cutthroat. The Miller Creek Trail heads east off the Lamar River Trail about a mile southeast of Calfee Creek, following Miller to its headwaters below Hoodoo Peak in the Absaroka Range.

Anglers report very high landing rates and excellent satisfaction with their over-all experience. The upper Lamar River drainage was severely affected by the fires of 1988. While some maps suggest that Miller Creek was not affected, it might be wise to check its status before planning a trip.

Mist Creek

A tributary of Cold Creek, supporting a population of pan-size cutthroat. The Mist Creek Trail cuts south off the Lamar River Trail at Cold Creek, following Mist through Mist Creek Pass then continuing down into Pelican Valley.

Mist Creek, Cold Creek, and Pelican springs were all affected by the fires of 1988. Check on the recovery status of the area before planning a trip. The Cold Creek patrol cabin is located about $1/2$ mile before the Cold Creek confluence on the west side of the Lamar.

Opal Creek

A tributary of the Lamar River, occasionally fished for pan-size cutthroat near its mouth. Access is by way of the Lamar River Trail, about a mile southeast of the Soda Butte crossing.

Pebble Creek

A good trout fishery near Pebble Creek Campground, $9^1/2$ miles from the Northeast Entrance. Pebble Creek Trail follows the creek north, eventually looping back to the Northeast Entrance Road, just $1^1/2$ miles inside the park.

Pebble Creek contains cutthroat and rainbow trout averaging ten inches, with a landing rate approaching two fish per hour. It is awarded above average angler ratings for over-all experience, and size and number of fish caught. The upper waters of the creek support a good trout population, though of smaller size.

The Pebble Creek Trail provides vistas of some of the park's most spectacular scenery. However, it does pass through an area that was burned by the fires of 1988 (the northern reach of the trail), so you might want to check on recovery status before planning a trip.

Rose Creek

A cutthroat stream crossed by the Northeast Entrance Road near the Lamar Ranger Station.

Slough Creek

A fine cutthroat fishery and beautiful stream in a splendid setting. Slough is a major tributary of the Lamar River, joining it about three miles east of Tower Junction.

A spur road off the Northeast Entrance Road about four miles east of Tower Junction leads north to Slough Creek Campground. From the campground, the Slough Creek Wagon Trail follows the stream to the park boundary, though hikers heading for First Meadow are advised to begin their trek from the trailhead on the north side of the entrance road,east of the campground, in order to avoid a steep, difficult piece of trail.

Throughout most of its flow through the park, Slough Creek is a slow moving meadow stream, supporting a mix of cutthroat and rainbow trout that average twelve to fifteen inches. The lower section, however, from the Lamar confluence to just above the campground, is characterized by riffles and cascades. It is easy to access on foot and supports larger fish, but offers a lower catch rate for its more prevalent rainbow and rainbow hybrids.

The First Meadow stretch of Slough, a one-mile hike from the trailhead, is extremely peaceful, offering smaller but respectable cutthroat and a catch rate second only to that of the Yellowstone's Hayden Valley.

In the Second Meadow section of Slough, two hours further up the trail, the creek meanders through an alpine valley with views of the peaks of the Absaroka, Beartooth, and Washburn ranges.

Anglers have given Slough an excellent rating for fish caught in the less accessible areas, and for size of fish landed. The average size of fish in this stream is increasing as a result of catch and release regulations.

Soda Butte Creek

A very nice trout stream in a lovely valley, easily accessed throughout its park run by the Northeast Entrance Road between the entrance gate and the creek's confluence with the Lamar River.

Soda Butte offers fishing for cutthroat trout averaging over ten inches. Angler surveys on Soda Butte Creek indicate excellent satisfaction with the over-all experience, above average satisfaction with size and number of fish caught. The landing rate approaches two fish per hour.

Timothy Creek

Joins the Lamar River from the south about 2 $1/2$ miles upstream from the Miller Creek Trail junction. It offers fishing for pan-size cutthroat in its lower reaches.

Trout Lake

Heavily fished for rainbow and cutthroat, Trout Lake is located about one mile southwest of the Pebble Creek Campground, close to the Northeast Entrance Road. Watch for a vehicle turn-out on the west side of the road. There is no sign.

A half-mile trail leads to the lake, which is partially surrounded by hilly meadows that attract grazing buffalo. Mt. Hornaday is to the north.

Trout Lake receives heavy angling pressure, with catches averaging fourteen inches. Recent surveys indicate a landing rate of less than one fish per hour. Anglers give an above average rating to number of fish caught, size of fish landed, and to the over-all experience here.

Willow Creek

Enters the Lamar River from the south, about four miles upstream from the Miller Creek Trail junction. It offers fishing for pan-size cutthroat in its lower reaches.

Willow Creek joins the Lamar in an area that was severely scorched by the fires of 1988. Check the status of the area before planning a trip.

NATIONAL PARK SERVICE

ZONE 3

Headwaters of the Madison River, including the Gibbon and Firehole River watersheds.

This zone is dominated by the Gibbon and Firehole rivers, which join in National Park Meadow to create the Madison, only a small segment of which flows within Yellowstone Park.

The waters of the Firehole are warmed by numerous geothermal features, including Old Faithful and many lesser known geysers and springs. Bison and elk spend the entire year in the Firehole Valley and are sometimes seen in large numbers here.

The Gibbon River heads at Grebe Lake, where an angler willing to make the hike can still catch a grayling. Gibbon Meadows is usually home to an elk herd, and is a prime location for wildlife viewing.

The three major rivers of this zone are easily accessed by roads which parallel each of the streams. The West Entrance Road follows the Madison to Madison Junction, then tracks the Gibbon to Norris Geyser Basin. The Grand Loop Road follows the Firehole south from Madison Junction to Old Faithful.

Accommodations in this area are available at West Yellowstone outside the park, and at Old Faithful within the park. There are campgrounds at Madison Junction and Norris.

BILL WILLCOX

Much of the Firehole's best water is followed closely by the Grand Loop Road between Madison Junction and Old Faithful. The river supports populations of rainbow, browns, brook trout, and whitefish. The average size of the catch has dropped to nine inches in recent years, but some fish exceed eighteen inches.

including many pools, weed beds, and undercut banks.

Angler surveys report nearly one fish per hour caught on the Gibbon. Anglers express above average satisfaction with their experience, average satisfaction with the number of fish caught, but give below average rating for the size of fish caught. The biggest catches are taken below Gibbon Falls, and catch size (and angler pressure) progressively decrease up river, though more fish are landed in the upper sections.

The area through which the Gibbon flows was considerably affected by the fires of 1988. Check on the recovery status prior to planning a trip.

Goose Lake

A marginal fishery for rainbow trout averaging fourteen inches.

The 34 acre lake is located immediately east of Fountain Flats Freight Road, about 5 $1/2$ miles south of Madison Junction. A picnic area beside the lake provides access, and there are other opportunities to drive down to the lake. Goose has a small inlet and no outlet stream.

Angler satisfaction with the experience here is average, below average for numbers caught, and above average for the size of the fish. Landing rates have been very poor.

Gooseneck Lake

A small lake directly west of the Midway Geyser Basin. To reach it, follow directions to Goose Lake. The tributary that flows into the south end of Goose Lake is the Gooseneck Lake outlet. Follow the stream to Gooseneck. Gooseneck supports a population of rainbow trout that average eight inches.

Grebe Lake

Source of the Gibbon River, a big lake (156 acres) with a healthy population of rainbow trout and a catch and release fishery for plentiful grayling.

The lake can be reached by following the Ice Lake Trail north from Virginia Meadows. At Ice Lake, you can pick up the Howard Eaton Trail on Ice's north shore, and continue east past Wolf Lake to Grebe. A more direct route follows an old wagon road north from the Norris Canyon Road southwest of Canyon Village. Coming from the west, the old track cuts off less than a mile beyond a service road that branches off to the right. Grebe Lake, at elevation 8028 feet, is a very popular grayling fishery with good to excellent catches at times. The fish average eleven inches. Landing rates have been over one fish per hour. Anglers report above average satisfaction with their experience and with number and size of fish caught.

Grebe is in grizzly country, so keep an eye out and make lots of noise on the trail.

Iron Spring Creek

A small creek that empties into the Little Firehole near Old Faithful, a favorite refuge of the Firehole River's big trout during summer hot spells. Cooler than the Little Firehole, it supports resident populations of rainbow, brook, and brown trout averaging ten inches in length. When the Firehole approaches eighty degrees, many large fish move into this creek. They are extremely wary, however, and hard to catch.

Fishermen surveys indicate a landing rate approaching one fish per hour. Above average ratings are reported for angler satisfaction with their experience, numbers caught, and with the size of the fish.

The Iron Spring Creek area was severely affected by the fires of 1988. Check on the recovery status before planning your trip.

Little Firehole River

Tributary of the Firehole, entering the river just above the Biscuit Basin parking area, a mile or so below Old Faithful. Rainbow, brook, brown, and cutthroat trout averaging ten inches offer anglers above average satisfaction with their over-all experience, with number of fish caught, and size of fish.

Landing rates have been running under one fish per hour. The Little Firehole area was less affected by the 1988 fires than other streams in the Firehole drainage.

Madison River

Headwaters of one of the West's most famous fisheries. It is formed by the confluence of the Firehole and Gibbon rivers just fifteen miles inside the West Entrance of Yellowstone Park. The Madison then flows another 136 miles to Three Forks, Montana, where it meets the Gallatin and Jefferson to produce the Missouri River.

Easily accessed from the West Entrance Road throughout most of its National Park flow, it is heavily fished, though its wary and well-protected population elude many anglers who try their luck here. The Madison is restricted to fly fishing only.

Within the park the river supports large populations of brown trout, rainbow, and whitefish, as well as some cutthroat and brook trout. The resident fish vary greatly in size, even in this relatively short stretch, with many browns and rainbow over three pounds, and some enormous whitefish. Even larger fish migrate from Hebgen Lake to spawn in the Madison, enhancing the fishing potential. There are spring and fall runs of rainbow, a fall run of whitefish, and a famous fall run of brown trout.

There is a large campground and parking lot at the head of the river, known as Madison Junction. The many vehicle turn-outs between the Junction and the Western Entrance usually indicate worthy fishing. Near the Junction, the Madison flows through National Park Meadows, an extremely weedy stretch with many big holes and runs that have been known to hold very big fish.

As with many rivers beloved of fishermen, the Madison's best holes and drifts are lovingly (though unofficially) named. The big elbow in the National Park Meadow stretch is known as Big Bend (site of a huge deep hole, best fished with heavy nymphs). Nine Mile Hole (nine miles from West Yellowstone, $4^1/_2$ miles from the entrance gate), is a very productive boul-der-filled quarter mile stretch with deep water, gravel bars, and thick weed beds, best fished with dry flies. Downstream, (after a two mile flow between treacherously swampy banks) is Seven Mile Run, which begins just above the bridge. Seven Mile is characterized by weedy channels, downed trees, big

Creek the Nez Perce no longer sustains fish life due to high temperatures and acidic water.

Angler surveys indicate below average satisfaction with the over-all experience here, with number of fish caught, and with size of the fish. Landing rates are below one fish per hour.

Solfatara Creek

A tributary of the Gibbon, joining the river at Norris Junction near the Norris Ranger Station. Access is provided by the Solfatara Creek Trail, which begins near the station. There are fine meadows in the headwaters area.

Brook trout averaging nine inches provide a landing rate of under one fish per hour. Anglers give the creek an excellent rating for number of fish landed. Angler satisfaction with over-all experience and size of fish is average.

Spring Creek

Enters the Firehole River several miles east of Old Faithful. From the Grand Loop Road heading towards West Thumb, you will see Spring Creek, a small stream, on your right. It supports a small population of brook trout and a few brown trout, offering fair fishing.

Spruce Creek

A tributary of Nez Perce Creek, entering Nez Perce from the south about $1\frac{1}{2}$ miles upstream from the Magpie Creek confluence. It offers fair fishing for pan-size brook, brown, and rainbow trout.

West Fork

A small mountain stream that flows into Iron Spring Creek near its confluence with the Little Firehole. It contains small rainbow and brown trout, and offers only fair fishing.

White Creek

A small stream located along the Fountain Paint Pot scenic loop off the Grand Loop Road mid-way between Lower and Mid-way geyser basins. It has a population of brown trout that can provide some good fishing action.

Wolf Lake

A good rainbow and grayling fishery in the Gibbon River drainage southwest of Grebe Lake. Wolf can be reached by way of the Howard Eaton Trail from trailheads on Norris Canyon Road or from the Grebe Lake Trail.

The lake covers about fifty acres and is thirty-two feet deep. It is sourced and drained by the Gibbon, with inlet streams on the north shore that offer additional fishing opportunities, and several springs. It is attractively set among big meadows and pine forest.

Anglers give Wolf an excellent rating for over-all experience and number of fish caught. Fish average about eleven inches, with a landing rate of just under one fish per hour.

Wolf Lake is in grizzly country, so keep an eye out.

Alum Creek

 Tributary of the Yellowstone, with a resident population of small cutthroat. It is currently closed to angling to protect spawning grounds. Alum is crossed by the Canyon-Fishing Bridge Road.

Bluff Creek

 Tributary of Sour Creek. It offers fair to good fishing for small cutthroat trout.

Bog Creek

 Tributary of Sour Creek. Like its neighbor, Bluff Creek, it offers fair to good fishing for small cutthroat trout.

Cascade Creek

 Outlet of Cascade Lake, offering good fishing for cutthroat trout. See Cascade Lake for directions.

Cascade Creek cutthroat average ten inches. Angler surveys report above average satisfaction with over-all fishing experience and with number of fish caught, but only average satisfaction with size of fish. Cascade Lake offers catch-and-release fishing for cutthroat and grayling.

The Cascade Creek area was razed by the fires of 1988. Check on the status of recovery before planning a trip.

Cascade Lake

 A popular lake in the Canyon Junction area, with catch-and-release fisheries for cutthroat trout and grayling.

There are two trails to the lake, each $2^1/_2$ miles long. The Cascade Creek Trail follows the lake's outlet stream (Cascade Creek) from a trailhead $^1/_2$ mile west of Canyon Junction. A second trail heads at the picnic area about one mile north of Canyon Junction. Cascade Creek Trail offers the more scenic route.

The lake covers thirty-six acres, with a maximum depth of twenty-seven feet. There is a small inlet stream at the east end of the lake in a heavily forested area. The inlet is a gathering place for spawning grayling in early June.

Cascade receives very heavy angling pressure, but yields over one fish per hour. Anglers report excellent satisfaction with over-all experience, and above average satisfaction with size and number of fish landed. Catch-and-release management has increased angler satisfaction ratings in all categories.

Cascade is in grizzly country. Hikers are advised to inquire at a ranger station for reports of bear sightings, travel in groups of four or more, and obey bear area precautions.

This area was burned during the fires of 1988. Check on the status of recovery before planning a trip.

Cottongrass Creek

A small tributary of the Yellowstone entering the river from the east and crossed by the Howard Eaton Trail. It supports a resident population of pan-size cutthroat, but is closed to angling to protect spawning grounds.

Elk Antler Creek

Tributary of the Yellowstone with a resident population of small cutthroat. It is currently closed to angling to protect spawning grounds. Elk Antler is crossed by the Canyon-Fishing Bridge Road.

Sour Creek

A good cutthroat stream crossed by the Howard Eaton Trail about two miles from the trailhead near Canyon.

Thistle Creek

Tributary of the Yellowstone, entering the river from the east in the vicinity of LeHardy Rapids. It is crossed by the Howard Eaton Trail. Thistle offers fair angling for pan-size cutthroat trout.

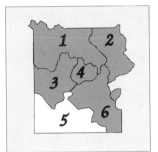

ZONE 5

*All park waters
on the west slope
of the Continental Divide*

Rich in scenic and angling treasures, this zone includes three major lakes (Lewis, Shoshone, and Heart) and four rivers (Lewis, Bechler, Falls, and Snake).

Shoshone Lake is the largest backcountry lake in the lower forty-eight states, and the most popular backcountry destination in the park. Canoeists make the trip by way of the Lewis Channel, which connects Shoshone with Lewis Lake. Lewis is the third largest lake in Yellowstone.

Bechler, Falls, and Snake rivers are all hike-in fisheries. Bechler and Falls are in the park's far southwest corner, known as "Cascade Corner." Here you will find twenty-one of the Park's forty-one waterfalls.

The elevation in this zone is lower, the climate wetter, the meadows thick with vegetation (and mosquitos). The Snake River area is summer home to a great many elk. There are extensive meadows, and vistas to the east of the jutting peaks of the Absarokas. Wildlife here is varied and plentiful, including bear, deer, elk, moose, sandhill cranes, and great blue herons

The Bechler and Falls River areas are accessed by Cave Falls and Reclamation roads, east of Ashton Idaho. The South Entrance Road approaches the Snake River and Lewis Lake. There are campgrounds at Lewis Lake and South Entrance.

ZONE 5

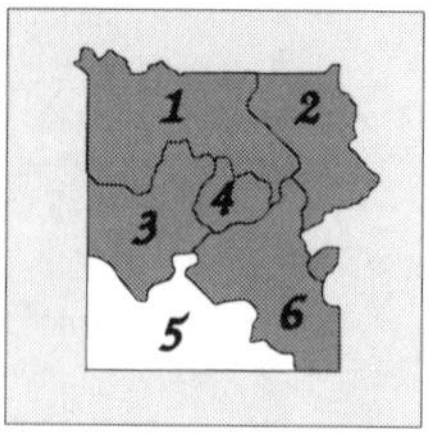

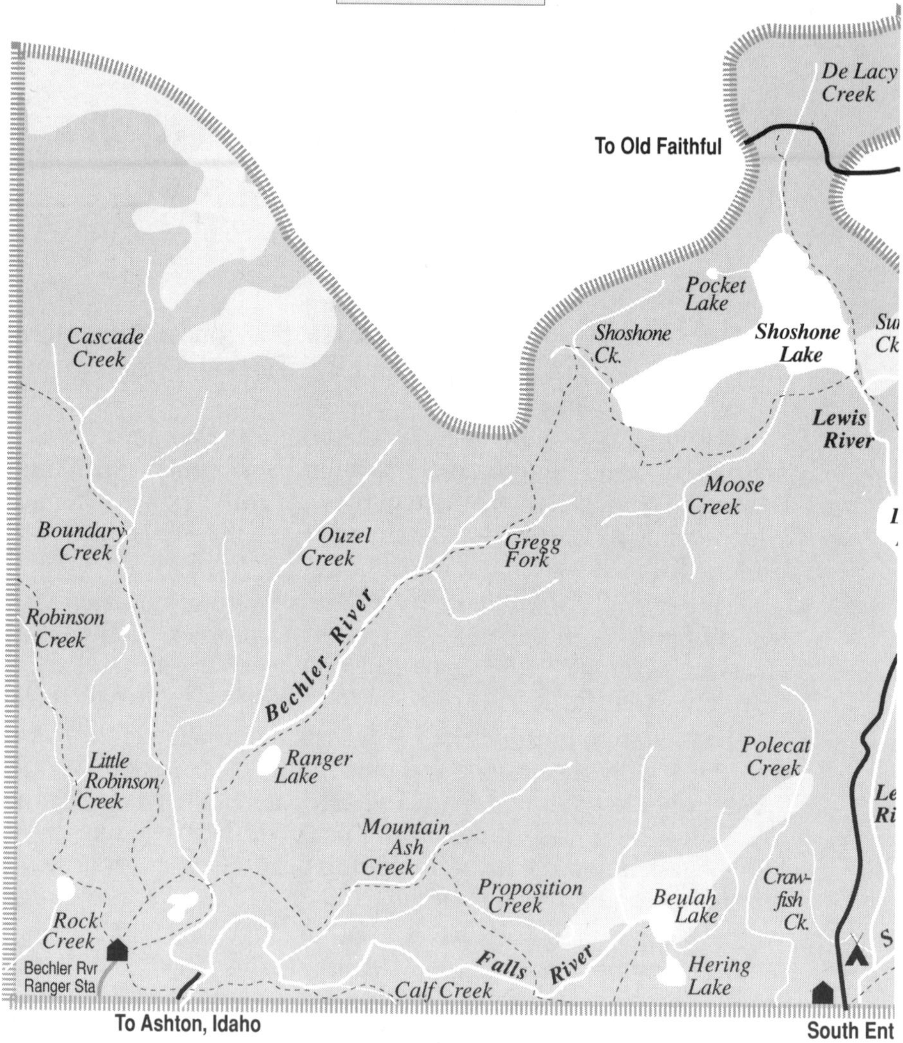

De Lacy Creek

To Old Faithful

Pocket Lake

Shoshone Ck.

Shoshone Lake

Su Ck.

Cascade Creek

Lewis River

Moose Creek

Boundary Creek

Ouzel Creek

Gregg Fork

Robinson Creek

Bechler River

Little Robinson Creek

Ranger Lake

Polecat Creek

Le Ri

Mountain Ash Creek

Proposition Creek

Beulah Lake

Craw-fish Ck.

Rock Creek

Bechler Rvr Ranger Sta

Falls River

Calf Creek

Hering Lake

S

To Ashton, Idaho

South Ent

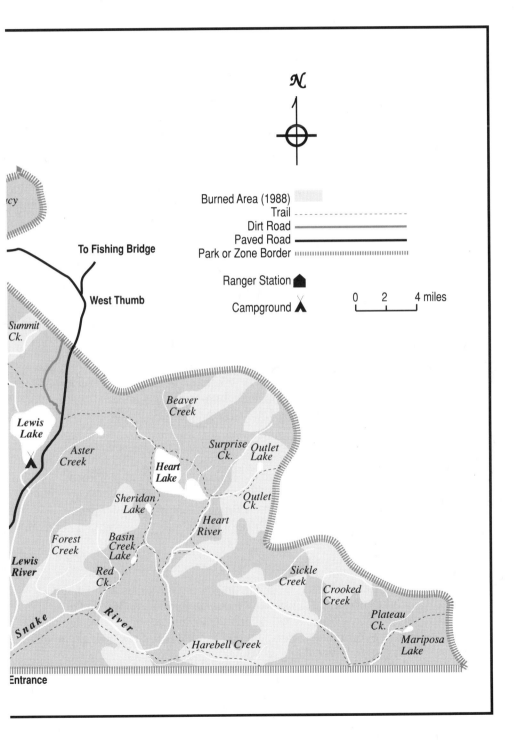

N

Burned Area (1988)
Trail
Dirt Road
Paved Road
Park or Zone Border

Ranger Station
Campground

0   2   4 miles

To Fishing Bridge

West Thumb

Summit
Ck.

Beaver
Creek

Lewis
Lake

Aster
Creek

Surprise
Ck.

Outlet
Lake

Heart
Lake

Outlet
Ck.

Sheridan
Lake

Heart
River

Forest
Creek

Basin
Creek
Lake

Lewis
River

Red
Ck.

Sickle
Creek

Crooked
Creek

Plateau
Ck.

Snake

River

Mariposa
Lake

Harebell Creek

Entrance

Aster Creek

A tributary of the Lewis River, providing fair fishing for small brook and brown trout. It joins the Lewis River just below Lewis Falls. Access to the stream can be found along the South Entrance Road just below Lewis Lake. Catch rates of under one fish per hour are reported.

Aster flows through an area that burned in 1988. Check on recovery status prior to planning a trip.

Basin Creek

An upper tributary of the Snake, fished for small cutthroat trout. Heart Lake Trail crosses the creek between Basin Creek Lake and Sheridan Lake. Other trails heading north from South Boundary Trail lead to the creek's lower waters.

Basin Creek Lake

A small lake on the west side of the Heart Lake Trail, about five miles south of Heart. It covers eight acres and has a maximum depth of seventeen feet. Its population of small cutthroat trout provides fair to good fishing.

Beaver Creek

Crossed by the Heart Lake Trail near Heart Lake's north shore, 1 1/2 miles east of Heart Lake Patrol Cabin . It supports a population of pan- size cutthroat trout. Anglers report a catch rate of over one fish per hour.

Bechler River

A medium-size river, primarily a hike-in fishery for good sized cutthroat and rainbow trout. It joins Falls River at the end of Cave Falls Road. A trail follows the river from that point, eventually joining the Bechler River Trail, which heads at Bechler River Ranger Station.

To reach the main trailhead, take Highway 47 to Cave Falls Road, then follow the ranger station cut-off. There is a parking lot for vehicles beside the trailhead.

The trail crosses a small stream and then forks at a pond (frequented by deer). Take the upper fork and, after about three miles of easy hiking, you will reach Bechler Meadows. To the north you can see Ouzel Falls. Moose, elk, deer, and sandhill cranes are frequently encountered in the upper meadow, and you may even get an opportunity to glimpse the rare whooping crane. Check the birder's logbook at the ranger station for latest sightings prior to hiking in.

The meadows area is usually very wet until late August, and the mosquitoes and flies can be thick. Be prepared.

Bechler's larger trout are found in the lower section of the river, from the upper meadows to the Falls River confluence. The average catch is about ten inches. Anglers often start fishing in the upper meadows where the trail crosses the river, then fish downstream to the confluence of Boundary Creek.

Bechler is clear and deep, requiring caution when wading. There are undercut banks and many deep holes that provide concealment for large trout. Bechler is a challenging river to fish, though it can provide good to excellent angling.

If you continue along Bechler River Trail from the upper meadows, you will enter the Bechler Canyon and soon reach Colonade Falls. There is a large pool beneath the falls that is worth fishing.

Angler success seems to have declined in recent years, and the frequency of large fish reports has decreased. However, anglers are still landing over one fish per hour, and surveys indicate above average satisfaction with over-all experience and number of fish landed. Satisfaction with catch size is below average. Most of the pressure on the river occurs in the Bechler Meadows area below Colonade Falls. Angler success is greater above the falls, but the fish are smaller.

Beula Lake

Headwaters of the Falls River, one of two nice backcountry cutthroat lakes near the park's south boundary. See also Hering Lake. Beula is approximately 107 acres, with a maximum depth of 36 feet.

The trail to Beula begins near the inlet of Grassy Lake in the Teton National Forest just south of the park. To reach the trailhead from the South Entrance, drive south to Reclamation Road (Ashton-Flagg), about two miles. The turn-off is near the Flagg Ranch by the Huckleberry Springs turn-off. This road is primitive and unmaintained, but passable for most passenger cars (not suitable for large RVs, however). Follow Reclamation Road to Grassy Lake parking area, where the trailhead is marked.

There are inlets on the north and south shores of the lake. The largest south shore inlet flows out of nearby Hering Lake.

Anglers give an excellent rating to Beula for over-all experience and number of fish caught. Size of fish landed is rated above average, with landing rates of over two fish per hour reported. Beula Lake fish average about eleven inches.

Boundary Creek

A tributary of the Bechler River, offering good fishing for cutthroat and rainbow trout. The upper waters of the creek are followed by Boundary Creek Trail (which leads to Buffalo Lake). A lower stretch can be accessed from the Bechler River Trail. This trail crosses Boundary just before its confluence with Bechler River at the lower end of Bechler Meadows. The meadows portion of either trail is usually very wet until later in the season (normally late August), and the mosquitoes and flies can be atrocious, so take plenty of repellent.

Boundary Creek contains cutthroat and rainbow trout that average nine inches, with landing rates of over one fish per hour. Anglers report above average satisfaction with over-all experience and with number of fish caught, average satisfaction with size.

The upper stretch of Boundary Creek includes the beautiful Dunada Falls, a 150 foot drop, and Silver Scarf Falls, a 250 foot cascade. There are also interesting geothermal features along the Boundary Creek Trail, and attractive wilderness vistas on the way to Buffalo Lake.

Calf Creek

A small stream accessed by the South Boundary Trail east of Cave Falls. It supports cutthroat and rainbow trout.

Cascade Creek

Tributary of Boundary Creek, supporting cutthroat and rainbow trout. Following the Boundary Creek Trail to the headwaters region, Cascade Creek is the first tributary to join Boundary Creek.

Crawfish Creek

Crossed by the South Entrance Road just north of the entrance. It contains a small population of cutthroat trout offering fair fishing. Anglers report catch rates of over one fish per hour.

Crooked Creek

Tributary of the Snake River which drains the land east of Barlow Peak. It is reached by the Snake River Trail. Crooked joins the Snake from the north about three miles from the park's southern border. Small cutthroat trout provide fair to good fishing.

DeLacy Creek

An inlet of Shoshone Lake, with good fishing for pan-size brown and brook trout. A trail follows the creek all the way to Shoshone from a trailhead in DeLacy Park, just east of Craig Pass on the road between Old Faithful and West Thumb. Catch rates of over two fish per hour have been reported.

Falls River

A steeply flowing river, punctuated with many cascades, offering good to excellent fishing. It flows about thirty-one miles through the park's southwest boundary area. Bechler River joins Falls just above the dead-end Cave Falls Park Road. The best fishing requires a hike.

Access to Falls River is by way of the South Boundary Trail, which parallels the South Boundary of the park from the Idaho side of the park to the South Entrance. To reach the trailhead from the west, follow Reclamation Road on the Idaho side to Ashton, Idaho. At the east end of town, turn right onto Highway 32, then left at the Reclamation turn-off. About forty miles of dirt road leads to Flagg Ranch, which is located just outside the South Entrance to the Park. From the Wyoming side, the turn-off is marked by the Huckleberry Hot Springs sign just north of Flagg Ranch, where you will turn left and remain on the road towards Grassy Lake Reservoir. The road is primitive and poorly maintained, passable for most passenger cars, but not for large RVs. Seldom used, this road offers a very scenic view of the area. The headwaters of Falls River can also be approached from Beula Lake.

Angler success catching cutthroat and rainbow trout increases the further upstream you go, and the fishing pressure also decreases. Falls Creek is a popular stream with local fly anglers.

The frequency of catching larger trout, sixteen to twenty inches, appears to be declining, which may necessitate new regulations. Most recent angler surveys indicate a landing rate of under one trout per hour, average satisfaction with the over-all experience and with the number of fish landed, and below average satisfaction with size of fish caught.

Forest Creek

A tributary of the Snake River that joins the Snake from the north about four miles along the South Boundary Trail that begins at the South Entrance. It supports a population of pan-size cutthroat trout that provide good fishing.

Forest Creek flows through an area that was affected by the fires of 1988. Check on recovery status prior to planning a trip.

Gregg Fork

One of the headwaters of the Bechler River. It contains a pop-ulation of cutthroat trout.

Harebell Creek

Follows the South Boundary Trail in the vicinity of Harebell Patrol Cabin near the junction with Basin Creek Trail. It has a population of cutthroat trout.

Heart Lake

A large hike-in lake, with productive fisheries for cutthroat and lake trout, and some mountain whitefish. It covers about 2150 acres, with a maximum depth of 180 feet.

The Heart Lake Trailhead is on the east side of the South Entrance Road, just northeast of Lewis Lake (across from the Lewis-Shoshone Channel trailhead). The hike in is about eight miles, passing some interesting geothermal features.

Very large lake trout and some lunker cutthroat are caught here each year. The cutthroat average sixteen inches. Boats with motors are not allowed, so most of the fishing is done from shore. The lake trout are in shallow water early and late in the season, but go deep after the weather warms. A popular method of fishing the lake is to wade out in chest waders as far as you can, then cast heavy lures and allow them to settle as close to the bottom as possible before retrieving. Look for structure (an area affording fish food and/or shelter), where a drop off is evident, especially near a feeder stream, and you may be surprised by the results. The largest lake trout every caught in the Park was caught here (forty-three pounds). Fly fishermen do very well casting to rising fish.

Heart Lake is a hiking destination, and the pressure is not as heavy as at the more accessible lakes and streams. Landing rates reported were under one fish per hour. Most angler surveys show above average satisfaction with the over-all experience and with number and size of fish.

Heart River

A short river formed by the outlet stream at the southeast corner of Heart Lake. It flows about four miles before joining the Snake. The upper three miles are followed closely by the Heart River Trail. The river supports a population of cutthroat trout that sustains a catch rate of over one fish per hour.

Hering Lake

One of two nice backcountry cutthroat lakes near the park's south boundary. See Beula Lake for road and trail directions. To reach Hering, follow the broadest inlet on Beula's south shore.

Lewis Lake in a boat and then following the channel upstream. After it leaves Lewis Lake, the river is paralleled by the South Entrance Road, which provides immediate access.

The average size of fish landed is around fourteen inches, with a landing rate under one per hour. Angler satisfaction with the experience, size of fish caught and the number of fish landed is above average. The large brown trout below Lewis Lake are more difficult to catch.

Little Robinson Creek

Tributary of Robinson Creek. See Robinson Creek for directions. Little Robinson is crossed by the West Boundary Trail immediately before its confluence with Robinson west of Bechler River Ranger Station. It offers fair fishing for small brook trout.

Mariposa Lake

A long hike in for rainbow and cutthroat fishing. Follow the South Boundary Trail about twenty-eight miles from the South Entrance of the park. The fish average ten inches, with a landing rate over one fish per hour. Anglers express excellent satisfaction with the over-all experience and with number of fish caught, above average satisfaction with catch size.

Moose Creek

An inlet of Shoshone Lake, on the south shore about two miles west of Shoshone Lake Ranger Station. The Shoshone Lake Trail heading west from the ranger station provides access. Moose Creek supports populations of small brown and brook trout, with catch rates of just under two fish per hour.

Mountain Ash Creek

An excellent cutthroat and rainbow fishery, tributary of Falls River. It is reached by the Old Marysville Road Trail, which forks off the lower Bechler Falls Trail (skirting the east shore of Lilypad Lake). Angler surveys indicate a landing rate of nearly one fish per hour with excellent satisfaction with number and size of fish caught.

Outlet Creek

Outlet of Outlet Lake, which perches above Heart Lake about three miles east. Outlet Creek flows south to join Surprise Creek, which empties into the Heart River a quarter mile from its source at the outlet of Heart Lake. The creek is crossed by the Heart Lake Trail. Its pan-size cutthroat trout offer fair to good fishing.

Outlet Lake

A tiny lake perched above Heart Lake, offering fair fishing for small cutthroat trout. At an elevation of 7749 feet, it covers sixteen acres, with a maximum depth of five feet.

To reach it, follow the Heart Lake Trail toward the Heart River outlet at the southeast tip of the lake. Outlet Creek flows into the river from the northeast. Follow the creek to Outlet Lake.

Ouzel Creek

A tributary of the Bechler River, offering fair fishing for pan-size rainbow and cutthroat trout. Ouzel Creek empties into the Bechler at the upper end of the Bechler Meadows, a wonderful area to observe wildlife. To the north, you can see Ouzel Falls. There are no fish in the stream above the falls.

Plateau Creek

Near the junction of the Chipmunk Creek Trail and the South Boundary Trail. It has a population of cutthroat trout.

Pocket Lake

A fourteen acre off-trail lake above Shoshone Lake, with a population of cutthroat trout that provide fair fishing. To reach Pocket, follow the Pocket Creek outlet, which is crossed by the Shoshone Lake Trail. From the DeLacy/Shoshone Trail junction, follow the Shoshone Lake Trail west to the outlet. Pocket has a maximum depth of twenty-four feet.

The lake has been involved in a cutthroat restoration project, and the previous population of brook trout has been eliminated. Recent surveys suggest this lake, at elevation 8100 feet, may be a marginal habitat to sustain a viable population of cutthroat trout.

Polecat Creek

Accessed at Moose Falls just north of the South Entrance on the South Entrance Road. Polecat offers fair fishing for small cutthroat trout.

Proposition Mountain Creek

A small tributary of Mountain Ash Creek, crossed by the Marysville Road Trail about one mile east of the Union Falls Trail junction. It offers good fishing for pan-size cutthroat and rainbow.

Ranger Lake

Located near the Bechler River in the southwest corner of the park. Rainbow trout were introduced during stocking operations, but no information is available as to the present status of the fishery.

Red Creek

Tributary of the Snake, supporting pan-size cutthroat. The Heart Lake Trail follows Red Creek after fording the Snake about six miles from the South Entrance. See Heart Lake for directions.

Robinson Creek

A mountain stream offering good fishing for small brook and brown trout. Robinson is crossed by the West Boundary Trail, heading at the Bechler River Ranger Station in the far southwest corner of the Park. To reach the station, turn off Highway 47 onto Cave Falls Road, then follow the turn-off to the ranger station (Cave Falls Road dead-ends at the falls).

Robinson Creek is the first stream you cross after passing Robinson Lake and is about three miles from the ranger station.

Rock Creek

Outlet of Robinson Lake, offering some fishing for pan-size brook trout. See Robinson Lake for directions. Follow the lake's south shore to reach the outlet.

Sheridan Lake

A small, shallow lake about one mile south of Heart Lake, accessed by the Heart Lake Trail. Sheridan covers about 15 acres and is only five feet deep. It offers fair fishing for cutthroat trout.

Shoshone Creek

A small mountain stream that flows into the west end of Shoshone Lake. It can be found by hiking along the Shoshone Lake Trail approximately eight miles from the trailhead near Old Faithful. Small brown and brook trout provide good fishing, with reported catch rates of over one fish per hour.

Shoshone Lake

The largest backcountry lake in the lower forty-eight states, and second largest lake in the park. It receives little fishing pressure in comparison with more accessible lakes, but it is the most popular backcountry destination in Yellowstone. Shoshone covers about 8050 acres, with a maximum depth of 205 feet.

The lake is closed to motorized craft, but canoeing around Lewis Lake and up the Lewis-Shoshone Channel is a popular approach. Canoeists are urged to follow the Lewis Lake shoreline rather than head across the lake, in deference to precocious and powerful winds that can pick up at any time. The channel can be paddled most of the way, with a tow line or portage required for the final mile. More portaging and pulling are required in later summer and fall. Like Lewis, Shoshone, has a reputation for sudden storms, so use caution in your explorations.

Trails leading into Shoshone include the Howard Eaton Trail, DeLacy Creek Trail and the Lewis-Shoshone Channel

Trail. The Channel Trail heads off a primitive road just north of Lewis Lake, across the road from the Heart Lake trailhead. It is a 4½ mile hike to the south end of Shoshone, where there are designated campsites. The DeLacy Creek Trail heads south from the Grand Loop Road at DeLacy Park, between Old Faithful and West Thumb (9½ miles east of Old Faithful). It is about three miles to the lake, seven to the channel. It is a longer route to the lake on the Howard Eaton Trail heading south from Old Faithful, or by way of the Bechler River Trail which begins at the South Entrance.

Once there, anglers will find that brown trout and lake trout are most prevalent, with some brook trout also available. Most of the trout caught average seventeen inches, but larger lake trout are caught at times. In the late fall the brown trout become extremely aggressive, and angler success achieves an excellent rating for those willing to chance the frequent fall storms. During the summer, if you want lake trout you will have to troll deep, but in the spring and fall they are often found in shallower water. The south shore of the lake seems more popular with successful fisherman.

Landing rates of under one fish per hour are reported by anglers, with those fishing from shore having a significantly greater landing rate than boat fishermen. Angler satisfaction with their over-all experience, size of fish caught, and number caught is above average to excellent.

Sickle Creek

Tributary of the Snake River which drains the land east of Chicken Ridge. It is reached by the Snake River Trail. Small cutthroat trout provide fair to good fishing.

Snake River

The Snake River wanders over forty miles along the south boundary of the park. It is reached only by trail except for the small section near the South Entrance. Because access requires long hikes, the Snake does not receive the fishing pressure other park waters often do.

There are several trails that follow the river, beginning with the South Boundary Trail, which heads near the South Entrance

Ranger Station. To reach the headwaters, follow the trail about eleven miles from the entrance, then take the Basin Creek Trail for three miles to the Heart River Trail. Remain on the Heart River Trail for seven miles to the Big Game Ridge Trail. Follow this trail east until you come again to the South Boundary Trail, which follows the headwaters to their source.

Cutthroat and whitefish make up the biggest share of the fish population, with some brook, lake, brown, and rainbow also available. The fish average eleven inches, with landing rates under one fish per hour. Anglers give above average ratings for the over-all experience, average for number of fish caught, and above average for size of fish landed. Landing rates appear to be declining when compared with previous years. This stream seems to be producing far below its fishery potential and may require special regulations to restore quality fishing.

The Snake flows through some areas that were affected by the fires of 1988. Check on their recovery status prior to planning a trip.

Summit Creek

A small mountain stream that enters the Lewis River near the outlet from Shoshone Lake. It supports a population of small brook trout that provide limited fishing. The creek is crossed by the Channel Trail between Shoshone and Lewis lakes.

Surprise Creek

A tributary of Heart River, offering fair to good fishing for pan-size cutthroat trout. The creek joins the river near the Heart Lake outlet. See Heart Lake for directions. Surprise Creek is in an area that was affected by the fires of 1988. Check its recovery status prior to planning a trip.

TOM MURPHY

ZONE 6

That portion of the Yellowstone River watershed that includes Yellowstone Lake, from the park's southern boundary to a point one mile downstream from the lake outlet.

Glancing at a map of the park, it is Yellowstone Lake that draws the eye. Over twenty miles long and fourteen miles wide, it has an average depth of 139 feet and is 320 feet deep in places. Cupped in an ancient caldera at elevtion 7733 feet, the lake is cold the year around. Even insulated waders cannot protect anglers from its chill.

Cutthroat trout, however, thrive in this environment, and the lake is home to the largest inland cutthroat population in the world. Wildlife is abundant in the vicinity of the lake, including representatives of nearly every park species.

This zone also includes the marshy wilderness beginnings of the Yellowstone River, which pours into the lake's southeast arm.Though fifty percent of the park's angling activity takes place at Yellowstone Lake, very few anglers sample the lake's remote bays or explore its myriad inlet streams.

Only thirty miles of shoreline are accessible by car, following the West Thumb-Fishing Bridge Road and the East Entrance Road. The two main trail networks within the zone are the Thorofare Trail on the lake's east shore, and Trail Creek Trail in the south. Accommodations are available at Grant Village and Lake. There are campgrounds at Grant Village, Bridge Bay, and Fishing Bridge.

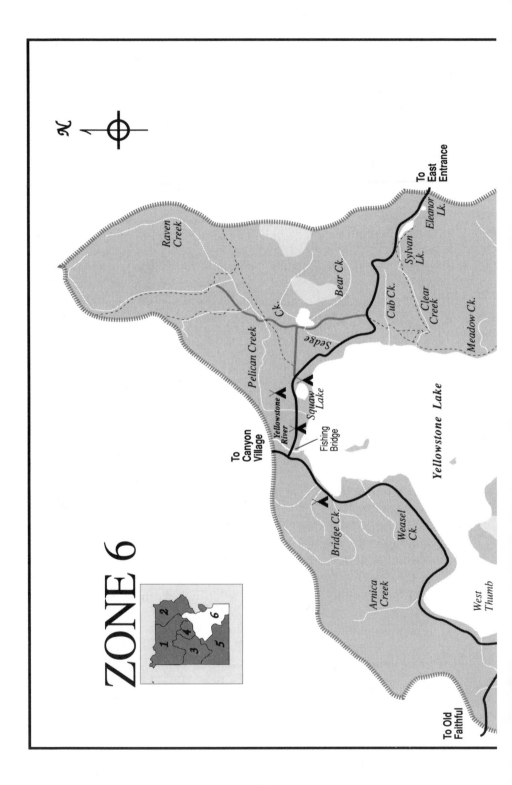

ZONE 6

Raven Creek

Bear Ck.

Sedge

Ck.

Pelican Creek

To Canyon Village

Yellowstone River

Fishing Bridge

Squaw Lake

Cub Ck.

Clear Creek

Sylvan Lk.

Eleanor Lk.

Meadow Ck.

To East Entrance

Yellowstone Lake

Bridge Ck.

Weasel Ck.

Arnica Creek

West Thumb

To Old Faithful

N

1 2 3 4 5 6

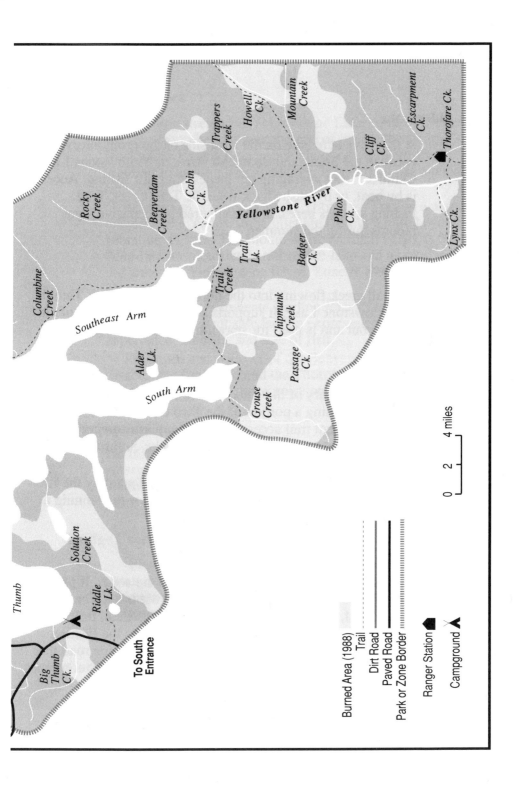

Thumb

Big Thumb Ck.

Solution Creek

Riddle Lk.

To South Entrance

Columbine Creek

Rocky Creek

Beaverdam Creek

Southeast Arm

Alder Lk.

South Arm

Grouse Creek

Passage Ck.

Chipmunk Creek

Trail Creek

Trail Lk.

Cabin Ck.

Trappers Creek

Howell Ck.

Mountain Creek

Badger Ck.

Yellowstone River

Phlox Ck.

Cliff Ck.

Escarpment Ck.

Thorofare Ck.

Lynx Ck.

Burned Area (1988)
Trail
Dirt Road
Paved Road
Park or Zone Border
Ranger Station
Campground

0   2   4 miles

by grizzly bears. A short trail here loops down to the Yellowstone River. See Yellowstone River, Zone 6, for directions to the trailhead.

Chipmunk Creek

Flowing west off Two Oceans Plateau into the South Arm of the lake, a spawning ground for Yellowstone Lake cutthroat.

Chipmunk is crossed by the Trail Creek Trail about a mile west of the Trail Creek Patrol Cabin. See Trail Creek for directions. A trail follows Chipmunk upstream several miles from the lake, before cutting west to follow Passage Creek.

Anglers report average satisfaction with the number of fish caught here and excellent satisfaction with the over-all experience and size of fish.

Chipmunk flows through an area that was affected by the fires of 1988. Check on the status of recovery prior to planning a trip.

Clear Creek

A major spawning stream for Yellowstone Lake cutthroat. To reach it, follow the Thorofare trail along the east shore of Yellowstone Lake two miles to the Clear Creek Trail junction. An old horse trail also comes in here, so be sure to look for official trail markers. Thorofare crosses Clear Creek about one mile beyond the junction.

The Clear Creek Trail can be followed from Sylvan Lake to Yellowstone Lake, a descent of some 700 feet. The trailhead is at the southeast end of Sylvan immediately east of the East Entrance Road. The trail follows the creek from the lake's west shore, through a meadow below Grizzly Peak, before entering dense forest.

Landing rates of over two fish per hour have been reported, with excellent angler satisfaction with over-all experiences, number of fish caught, and size.

Cliff Creek

A small cutthroat steam, tributary of the Yellowstone River in the upper Thorofare area. It is crossed by the Thorofare Trail about two miles north of the Thorofare Ranger station. The creek is a spawning stream for Yellowstone Lake cutthroat. Cliff flows through an area that was affected by the fires of 1988. Check on the status of recovery before planning a trip.

Columbine Creek

A spawning stream for Yellowstone cutthroat with a resident population of small trout. It is crossed by the Thorofare Trail about three miles south of the Park Point Patrol Cabin and flows into the lake near the wrist of the Southeast Arm, about a nine mile hike from the trailhead. See Yellowstone River, Zone 6, for directions to the trailhead.

Cub Creek

A spawning area for Yellowstone Lake cutthroat trout, with some smaller resident fish. Cub is crossed by the Thorofare Trail about 1 1/2 miles from the trailhead on the East Entrance Road. The Thorofare Trail follows the lake's east shore, then continues along the upper Yellowstone River.

Anglers report excellent satisfaction with their experience fishing Cub, with number of fish caught, and with size of the fish.

Eleanor Lake

A tiny shallow lake approximately one mile east of Sylvan Lake, just off the East Entrance Road. It somehow sustains a population of cutthroat trout that provides fair fishing. Anglers report a landing rate of under one fish per hour with above average satisfaction with the experience. Angler satisfaction with number and size of fish, however, is below average.

Escarpment Creek

A tributary of the upper Yellowstone in the Thorofare area. Escarpment joins the river north of the Thorofare Ranger Station just inside the south park boundary. It is crossed by the Thorofare Trail (mile 31.5). Escarpment supports a population of small cutthroat trout and is used as a spawning area for Yellowstone Lake cutthroat.

Escarpment flows through an area that burned in the fires of 1988. Check on the status of recovery before planning a trip.

Grouse Creek

A small stream flowing north off Chicken Ridge, emptying into the southern tip of the South Arm of Yellowstone Lake. It is crossed by the Trail Creek Trail about five miles west of the Chipmunk Creek Trail.

Small cutthroat trout are in residence here, and the stream is used as a spawning area by the lake cutthroat.

Grouse flows through an area that was affected by the fires of 1988. Check on the status of recovery before planning a trip.

Howell Creek

A major tributary of Mountain Creek, joining Mountain about four miles above the Mountain Creek Trail junction with the Thorofare Trail (Thorofare Trail mile 25). The Mountain Creek Trail follows Howell through Eagle Pass. Howell has a population of small resident cutthroat.

This area was affected by the fires of 1988. Check on the status of recovery before planning a trip.

Indian Pond (Squaw Lake)

A small lake about three miles east of Fishing Bridge along the East Entrance Road. It covers twenty-four acres, with a maximum depth of seventy-two feet. Fed primarily by underground springs, it provides scant spawning ground for its resident cutthroat, which are small and provide poor fishing. Past attempts at stocking the pond did not improve the fishing and were discontinued. Yellowstone Lake cutthroat probably enter the pond during high water.

Lynx Creek

A minor tributary of the Yellowstone River, flowing from the west and draining the southern portion of the Two Ocean Plateau. The South Boundary Trail follows Lynx Creek for several miles before the confluence.

Lynx supports a population of small cutthroat trout and is used by Yellowstone Lake cutthroat as spawning grounds.

Lynx flows through an area that was affected by the fires of 1988. Check on the status of recovery prior to planning a trip.

Meadow Creek

A tiny stream that flows into Yellowstone Lake near the Park Point Patrol Cabin on the Thorofare Trail. It has a resident population of small cutthroat and is a spawning area for the lake cutthroat.

Mountain Creek

A tributary of the upper Yellowstone in the Thorofare area, which serves as a spawning stream for Yellowstone Lake cut-throat. It is crossed by the Thorofare Trail (mile 26) and accessed by the Mountain Creek Trail, which heads northeast from Thorofare at mile 25. The Mountain Creek Trail follows Mountain Creek for about four miles before following Howell Creek north toward Eagle Pass.

In addition to the lake spawners, Mountain Creek supports a population of small resident cutthroat. For more information abut the Thorofare Trail, see Yellowstone River, Zone 6.

Passage Creek

A tributary of Chipmunk Creek, which flows into Yellowstone Lake's south arm, primarily a spawning season fishery. See Chipmunk Creek for directions.

Anglers report average satisfaction with number of fish caught and excellent satisfaction with the over-all experience and size of fish.

Passage Creek flows through an area that was affected by the fires of 1988. Check on the status of recovery prior to planning a trip.

Pelican Creek

A major spawning area for Yellowstone Lake cutthroat. Pelican offers good to excellent fishing for trout averaging fourteen inches.

Access to the stream is by a foot trail that begins east of Fishing Bridge across the road from Squaw Lake. The first two miles of the stream are closed to fishing, so plan accordingly if you follow the stream rather than take the trail. The Pelican Creek Trail hits the creek about six miles upstream, a three mile hike. Following the creek through the Pelican Valley, be aware that this is grizzly country. Keep alert and make noise on the trail.

Angler surveys indicate a landing rate of over one fish per hour. Anglers rate the over-all fishing experience and number of fish caught above average. Size of fish caught is rated excellent.

Angler use of this stream has declined since it was restricted to catch-and-release. Subsequent success rate, size, and number of trout caught have increased. Present trends suggest that angling pressure is again on the rise.

Phlox Creek

A minor tributary of the Yellowstone River, flowing from the west and draining a portion of the Two Ocean Plateau. There is no convenient trail access. Phlox supports a population of small cutthroat trout and is used as spawning grounds by Yellowstone Lake trout.

Phlox flows through an area that was affected by the fires of 1988. Check on the status of recovery prior to planning a trip.

Raven Creek

A small tributary of Pelican Creek offering good fishing for cutthroat trout. To fish the stream, follow the Pelican Creek Trail about seven miles to the Pelican Springs Patrol Cabin. See Pelican Creek for directions. Head west (left) at the trail junction. This trail crosses Raven in one mile, then continues on to a junction with the Pelican Cone Trail, and an old service road that comes out near Turbid Lake east of Fishing Bridge. (Turbid Lake holds no fish.) In spite of low landing rates, Raven Creek is given excellent satisfaction responses for over-all experience, number of fish, and size of fish caught.

The Pelican Creek area was affected by the fires of 1988. You may want to check on the status of recovery before planning a trip.

Riddle Lake

An easily accessed hike-in lake east of the South Entrance Road a little more than two miles south of Grant Campground. Intense fishing pressure decimated the lake's native cutthroat population, leading to a complete closure for two years. The lake is now open for catch-and-release fishing only.

Hikers should be aware that the Riddle Lake Trail is frequented by grizzly bears. Hike in groups of four or more, and make plenty of noise on the trail.

Rocky Creek

A tributary of Beaverdam Creek, joining Beaverdam about one mile upstream from Beaverdam's entrance into Yellowstone Lake. Like Beaverdam, Rocky serves as a spawning stream for Yellowstone Lake cutthroat and maintains a population of small resident cutthroat. See Beaverdam Creek and Yellowstone River, Zone 6, for complete trail directions.

Sedge Creek

A small creek that flows into Turbid Lake from the northeast, offering fair to good fishing for small cutthroat trout. Sedge also drains Turbid into Yellowstone Lake near Butte Springs Picnic Area. Turbid is a highly acidic geothermal lake that supports no fish.

Sedge Creek receives below average angler satisfaction responses for number of fish caught and over-all experience. Average satisfaction was reported for size of fish.

Solution Creek

The outlet of Riddle Lake, flowing about ten miles into the West Thumb of Yellowstone Lake.

To reach the upper creek, follow the Riddle Lake Trail, which heads east from the South Entrance Road a little more than four miles south of Grant Campground. It is a two mile hike to the lake. Solution drains out on the lake's east shore. The upper creek supports a population of small cutthroat.

The lower creek, inlet to Yellowstone Lake, can be reached by a three mile boat trip across West Thumb. The inlet is fished for spawning lake cutthroat.

Squaw Lake See Indian Pond.

Sylvan Lake

A narrow lake, nestled in dense forest, adjacent to the East Entrance Road just east of Sylvan Pass. It offers fair fishing for cutthroat trout averaging ten inches.

Because of its accessibility from the road (there is a picnic area on the northwest shore), it has received heavy angling pressure. A decline in fish population lead to the imposition of a catch-and-release restriction here. Size of catch and landing rate have subsequently increased.

There are two inlet streams, one entering from the northeast, the other from southeast. The outlet drains west into Clear Creek.

Anglers indicate average satisfaction with their over-all experience at Sylvan and with the number of fish caught, and above average satisfaction with size. The current landing rate is under two fish per hour.

Thorofare Creek

The highest tributary of the Yellowstone within the park. The Thorofare Trail crosses the creek in the vicinity of Thorofare Ranger Station, where a ranger is usually in residence throughout the summer.

Thorofare's cutthroat trout provide excellent fishing for

those willing to make the hike. Anglers report excellent satisfaction with the experience and the number of fish caught.
Landing rates approaching three fish per hour have been
reported.

Trail Creek

Inlet and outlet of Trail Lake, flowing about two miles from
the lake into the southern tip of the Southeast Arm of
Yellowstone Lake. Trail Creek Trail crosses the creek a mile
before fording the Yellowstone River and joining the
Thorofare Trail.

Trail Creek is a major access into the southern Yellowstone
Lake area. It begins at Heart lake Patrol Cabin, reached by
way of the Heart Lake Trail that heads on the South Entrance
Road across from Lewis Lake.

Trail creek supports a resident population of small cutthroat
trout and is used as a spawning area for Yellowstone Lake
trout.

Trail Lake

A shallow wilderness lake covering fifty-five acres, about one
mile southeast of the southern tip of the Southeast Arm of
Yellowstone Lake. Trail Creek Trail crosses Trail Lake's
outlet stream (Trail Creek) a little more than two miles east of
Trail Creek Patrol Cabin. Follow the creek to Trail Lake.
Anglers who have visited the lake give it an excellent rating
for over-all experience and fishing quality.

Trappers Creek

A spawning stream for Yellowstone Lake cutthroat, with its
own population of small trout. Trapper is about two miles
south of Cabin Creek, crossed by the Thorofare Trail (mile
23). See Yellowstone River, Zone 6, for directions to the
trailhead.

Weasel Creek

A small creek flowing into Yellowstone Lake about a mile and a half south of Natural Bridge. It supports a population of resident cutthroat trout and is used for spawning by the lake cutthroat.

Yellowstone Lake

The central feature of Yellowstone National Park, remnant of an enormous volcanic caldera, covering about 87,450 acres, with an average depth of 139 feet, maximum depth 320 feet.

Visitors can anticipate almost daily late morning winds out of the southwest, with waves whipped up to five or six feet. Boaters who swamp risk death from rapid hypothermia in the lake's chilly waters. Don't take chances—this lake has claimed more victims than the bears.

Though a variety of fish species have been introduced to the lake at one time or another, the only surviving species (other than some successful baitfish) are cutthroat trout. Yellowstone Lake supports the largest population of cutthroat trout in the world. The lake is currently managed with the primary objective of providing harvestable cutthroat for the park's wildlife—the bears, mink, and waterfowl.

The Yellowstone River is its major inlet, entering from the southeast and flowing out at the north. In addition, there are over 100 smaller tributaries. The lake is in a beautiful setting, with the Absaroka Range to the east and other handsome peaks and plateaus gracing every vista. A fine view of the lake and its environment is available at the Lake Butte Overlook just off the East Entrance Road

All roads into the park eventually lead to Yellowstone Lake, but only thirty miles of the shoreline are accessible to motor vehicles. The remaining eighty miles of shoreline can only be reached by boat or foot. The two primary trails that explore the shoreline and tributaries are the Thorofare Trail, following the lake's east shore, and the Trail Creek Trail, which accesses the south and southeast arms. The most popular route to this trail is by way of the Heart Lake Trail, which begins on the east side of the South Entrance Road just north of Lewis Lake. Few park visitors take advantage of these trails, which offer a true wilderness experience and access to the spawning streams of the lake's big cutthroat.

The average size of Yellowstone Lake cutthroat is close to fifteen inches, with many over twenty inches landed. Fishing here is primarily a catch-and-release proposition, since regulations restrict keeping to two fish under 13 inches, and there are comparatively few fish in Yellowstone under 13 inches! You'll hear few complaints, however, since these regulations are directly responsible for restoring the lake's original state of bounty after decades of depletion.

Yellowstone is fished from both boat and shore. Many shore anglers use dry flies to tempt the surface feeders found close to sand bars, rocky points, and at spring and creek inlets. A favorite shore fishing area is close to Bridge Bay Campground, where a sand bar and shallow water provide a natural cruising ground for hungry cutthroat. Most of the time, if the light is right and the air is calm, you can see the direction the fish are moving. A well-placed cast ahead of the fish can bring the slow, slurping strike of feeding trout.

But the advantage belongs to boating anglers, according to catch reports. There are public boat launches on the north and west shores, including full service marinas at Bridge Bay, Fishing Bridge, Grant Village, and Lake Village. Rental boats and guides are available at the marinas, as are canoe tows and ferries across the lake. Boaters must secure a Boat Permit. Anglers piloting their own craft should be wary of sudden severe weather changes and would be well advised to always stay within easy reach of shore. Be sure to read the boating regulations carefully, since portions of the lake are off limits to motorized craft.

Yellowstone Lake receives almost fifty per cent of the park's angler use. The northwest portion of the lake is most heavily fished, and the central and southern portions least fished.

The more remote areas of the lake provide a higher success rate and larger catch size. The average landing rate for the entire lake is over one fish per hour. The most recent angler survey report shows excellent satisfaction with the over-all experience and size of fish landed, and above average satisfaction with number of fish caught.

Yellowstone River

The wilderness section of the Yellowstone River, between the lake and the south boundary of the park. The area through which it flows is known as The Thorofare.

One popular access to the Thorofare is to hitch a ride on a boat to the Southeast Arm of Yellowstone Lake (charters are available), then join the Thorofare Trail to hike upriver. You can also hike into the area on the Thorofare Trail, which heads south from the East Entrance Road about a mile east of Yellowstone Lake. It is a twenty mile walk to the little loop trail that first leads down to Yellowstone River in the vicinity of the old Cabin Creek Patrol Cabin (removed after being destroyed by grizzly bears), and about thirty-one miles to Thorofare Ranger Station, just inside the south boundary of the park.

This is an incredibly scenic area, including the beautiful Yellowstone itself, as well as the huge meadows through which it winds, the impressive Two Ocean Plateau to the west, and the three Trident escarpments to the east.

Angler survey results for this portion of the river are of questionable reliability due to the small sample size, but of those received, satisfaction ratings are excellent for both number and size of fish caught (averaging sixteen inches). The number of available fish decreases rapidly after the spawning run, which is usually over by mid-August.

JIM VINCENT

FISHING DAY HIKES

This sampler of day hikes is recommended for those who want to escape the crowds and experienceYellowstone in its wild glory. Most visitors to Yellowstone (and most visiting anglers) do not hike. Even a two mile stroll will more than repay your efforts.

Before you head out, get a good trail map, and spend a little time talking to a park ranger. You'll get excellent advice and an update of trail conditions. For information about extended backcountry visits, see the bibliography at the end of this book.

Hellroaring Creek 3 miles   The trailhead is located 3.5 miles from Tower Junction on the Mammoth-Tower Road. The trail descends over 600 feet in the first mile to a suspension bridge over the Yellowstone River. At the two-mile mark there is a junction with the Yellowstone River Trail. When you see the patrol cabin you have reached the creek. A footbridge crosses the creek .5 miles further along the trail.

Yellowstone River, Seven Mile Hole 5.1 miles   The trailhead is located at Glacial Boulder, two miles from Canyon Village on the road to Inspiration Point. The trail follows the rim of the Grand Canyon, then descends to the river. The descent is fairly steep and requires strenuous effort on the way out, so be prepared.

Grizzly Lake 2 miles   The trailhead is located approximately one mile south of Beaver Lake on the Norris-Mammoth Road. The trail cuts through a meadow then climbs a steep hill and enters the forest. The lake is in a narrow valley surrounded by dense timber. The trail descends to the north end of the lake. Take plenty of repellent, for many mosquitoes inhabit this area.

Slough Creek 2 miles   The trailhead is about .5 miles before the Slough Creek Meadows Campground along the Northeast Entrance Road. The trail climbs gradually then descends into the open valley of Slough Creek. You'll find some patrol cabins by the creek and the junction for the Buffalo Plateau Trail. Fishing improves as you go upstream.

Trout Lake .5 miles   The trailhead is found on the north side of the Northeast Entrance Road about 1.8 miles south of Pebble Creek Campground. The trail climbs over a small ridge then continues to the lake. The hike is short and not very strenuous.

Grebe 3 miles   The trailhead is 4 miles west of Canyon Junction on the Norris-Canyon Road. The trail follows an old fire road most of the way. At the two-mile marker, take the trail that forks left. Be prepared to meet many mosquitoes if you go there before the middle of August.

Cascade Lake 2 miles   The trailhead is located .5 miles west of Canyon Village on the Norris-Canyon Road. The trail follows Cascade Creek and can be quite muddy until mid-July. Mosquitoes are prevalent, so bring repellent.

Bechler River Bridge 5 miles **Bechler Meadows** 3 miles   The shortest route begins at Bechler Ranger Station near the end of the Cave Falls Road about 25 miles from Ashton, Idaho. The trail is relatively flat and stays in the forest until you reach Boundary Creek Bridge and enter the meadows. You may be fortunate enough to see whooping cranes in the meadow in July.

In early summer the meadows are quite swampy and almost impossible to cross, so don't plan to hike there before July. You can follow the river and fish upstream if the meadows are muddy. If not, cross the meadows to the Bechler River Bridge and fish downstream. The mosquitoes and horse flies can be vicious, so take plenty of repellent.

Beula Lake 2.5 miles   The trailhead is at the eastern end of Grassy Lake Reservoir in Teton National Forest, Idaho. The trail is steep at first to the top of the ridge, then descends gradually to the shore of the lake.

Lewis-Shoshone Channel 4.5 miles   The trailhead is just north of Lewis Lake about 7 miles south of West Thumb Junction. A fishing trail forks from the main trail and follows the Lewis Lake shoreline to the channel. The trail is not steep and is easy to follow.

Shoshone Lake (via DeLacy Creek Trail 3 miles) (via LewisTrail 4.5 miles)   The DeLacy Creek trailhead is 8 miles east of Old Faithful on the West Thumb Junction Road near Craig Pass. It leads to a shallow portion of the lake and may not be the best choice in mid-summer if you want deep water.

The Lewis trailhead is on South Entrance Road, 7 miles south of West Thumb Junction. Neither trail is steep, and both are easy to follow.

Heart Lake 8 miles   The trailhead is on the South Entrance Road, 5.4 miles south of Grant Village near the north end of Lewis Lake. The first 5 miles of the trail are relatively level and easy to hike. The last 3 miles are mostly downhill to the shore of the lake. In the spring the trail is muddy but tolerable if you're wearing waterproof boots.

Pelican Creek 3 miles   Pelican Valley trailhead is on a spur road north of Squaw Lake, 3 miles east of Fishing Bridge. The trail leads to Pelican Creek Bridge then parallels the creek for 3 miles. The hike is relatively flat.

Yellowstone Lake, The Thorofare 3 miles   The trailhead is on the East Entrance Road approximately 10 miles east of Fishing Bridge. The first 1.5 miles are through forest, then the trail fords Cub Creek. At 2 miles you'll come to the Clear Creek Trail junction. Be sure to take the right fork, which leads to Clear Creek and the Fish and Wildlife fish trapping area. There is a footbridge over Clear Creek downstream from the trail.

McBride Lake 3 miles   The trailhead is on the east side of the dirt road that leads from the East Entrance Road to Slough Creek Campground, about .5 mile before the camp. Follow the Slough Creek Trail to its junction with the Buffalo Plateau Trail. Cross the creek following the Buffalo Plateau Trail, then head east across the meadows about one mile to a rocky forested area in which the lake is nestled. The ford across Slough Creek will be difficult if you attempt to cross before mid-July.

INDEX

INDEX

BIBLIOGRAPHY

Bach, Orville E. Jr. *Hiking the Yellowstone Backcountry.* San Francisco: Sierra Club Books, 1973.

Brooks, Charles E. *Fishing Yellowstone Waters.* Piscataway, NJ: Winchester Press, 1984.

Brooks, Charles E. "A Yellowstone Sampler". *Fly Fisherman,* June, 1981.

Fothergill, Chuck, and Sterling, Bob. *The Montana Angling Guide.* Aspen, CO: Stream Stalking Publishing Co., 1988.

Harrop, Rene. "Discovery in Yellowstone". *Fly Fisherman,* June, 1988.

Marschall, Mark C. *Yellowstone Trails.* Yellowstone Library and Museum Assoc., 1981.

Pierce, Steve. *The Lakes of Yellowstone.* Seattle: The Mountaineers, 1987.

Varley, John D., and Schullery, Paul. "Rivers Born and Brewed" *Fly Fisherman,* September, 1983.

ABOUT THE AUTHOR

Robert Charlton has fished the Yellowstone back country extensively, and been the source of many a "you should have been there yesterday" rumor in the Yellowstone area. His home on the banks of the Henry's Fork of the Snake River in St. Anthony, Idaho is well positioned for his frequent outings in the park.

Born in Utah, he received a Ph.D. in Professional Psychology from Utah State University. He subsequently moved to Idaho, where he lives with his wife, Linda, and their four children.